Full Circle

by Kathryn Stribling

Bilbo Books Publishing
ATHENS GEORGIA

Georgian Hotel, Athens, Ga

Marion and Kathryn's house in Habersham Mills

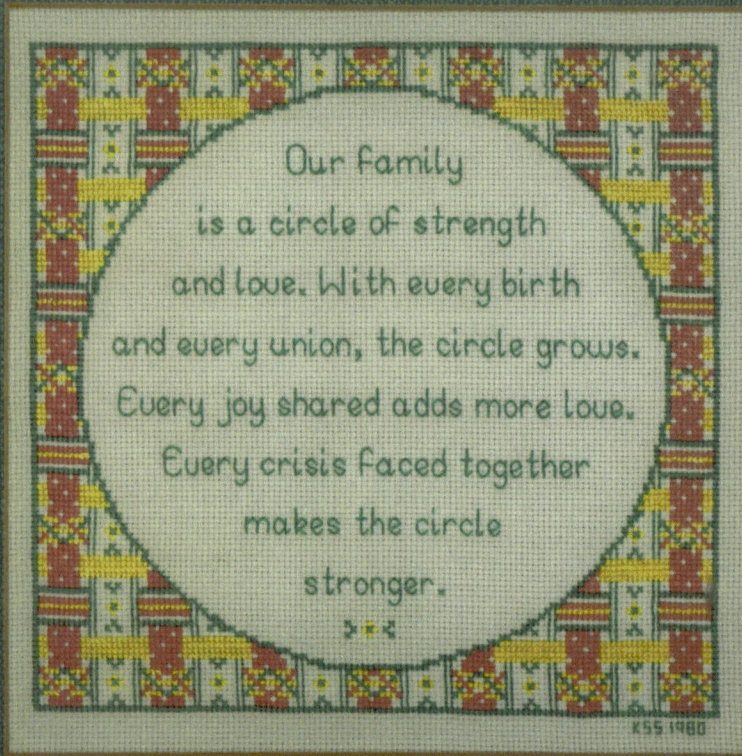

Needlework done by Kathryn, 1980

FULL CIRCLE

BY KATHRYN STILES STRIBLING

IN RURAL BALDWIN COUNTY, GEORGIA AT THE TURN OF THE century the major cash crop was, of course, cotton. Picking cotton is hard work. It's dangerous, too. For most of the week, people picked the cotton. Once a week the local farmers loaded their picked cotton into a wagon and wheeled it to my Uncle Hugh's cotton gin. Gins were expensive. Therefore, "Ginning Day" was a big deal for the county. All of the local farmers hauled that week's pickings to Uncle Hugh's farm and loaded it into the machine for processing. One "Ginning Day" in the cotton fields, the farmers and field hands of Baldwin County saw an eight-year-old boy's arm get utterly mangled in a cotton gin. Tagging along with his relatives to this semi-festive community event, the boy had followed his insatiable curiosity toward the giant, whirling contraption, mesmerized by the semi-industrial process. Raw cotton was run through a wooden drum embedded with a series of hooks that caught the fibers and dragged them through a mesh. The mesh was too fine to let the seeds through, but the hooks pulled the cotton fibers through with ease. After going through the gin, the cotton was clean. The raw cotton goes into the gin. It was a super-charged magnet for a curious young boy.

Peering in to see how the gin worked, the boy got too close

and was accidentally caught up in the machinery. His right arm was torn to shreds and he was rushed to the rather primitive regional hospital on horseback. Though they were unable to save the boy's right arm, this loss turned out to be a blessing in disguise for the boy. He turned what others would condescendingly call a "disability" into an advantage.

Feeling the need to constantly prove himself, becoming a more independent person in the process, the boy never let his lack of an arm impede his lofty ambitions. Years later, that boy attended Georgia Military College. He drove his own automobile. He required no assistance with anything he set his mind to. He turned a post-graduation night clerk job at The Baldwin Hotel in Milledgeville into a wildly successful career as a hotel magnate.

That boy was my father.

My maternal grandfather was a Methodist preacher, making my mother a "preacher's kid". When the Reverend Steven Henry Dimon, the new Methodist minister, with his four lovely daughters in tow, moved to Milledgeville, it was big news. The arrivals of new preachers used to excite Southern towns. Four beautiful, young, single girls still do. My mother, Mary Haygood Dimon, was a true beauty, with Gibson Girl looks and a stately manner. She and her equally-attractive sisters were always close. In fact, when my father asked my grandfather for his daughter's hand in marriage, he was warned, "You're not just marrying one daughter. You're marrying her sisters, too." He had a valid point. My mother and my aunts Taudie and Teal were always a large part of our family.

My parents were married during WWI in Milledgeville, in the middle of the night. My grandfather, the Methodist minister, performed the ceremony himself, in their home. They did not have to get married, but he had to get back to his job.

I, Kathryn Stiles Stribling, have led an interesting life.

I was born in the Roaring Twenties, in the decidedly less-than-roaring area of my grandparents' front bedroom in Toccoa, Georgia, on September 20, 1926.

Northeast Georgia is agricultural, pastoral, and partially mountainous. I was reared in the Appalachian foothills, where the farm meets the factory. My lifetime has seen America change from a primarily rural country to a more industrial society, from a sedentary nation where it was rare to travel more than a few miles from one's home on horseback to a land of mass transit, of interstate highways, and of international commerce. Being reared in the various hotels run by my father allowed me to see it all…and I did.

It's ironic that I was in the last generation of Americans to be born at home. In those days pregnant women didn't display their maternal status for all the world to see, like they do now. In fact, they did the exact opposite. If they were able to do so financially, the expecting women of the time mainly hid away from the world, resting, allowing the baby to mature to term in the womb, as my mother did. If I hadn't been born into a hotel family, my home birth wouldn't be at all ironic, but I was launched into a life on the move.

Probably the strongest illustration of the sense I'm talking about came in the person of Dr. Ayers, the man who delivered me, the only physician in Toccoa. His idea of a pre-natal exam was seeing women in church, calmly and patiently listening to their symptoms, and then patting their heads and predictably telling them, "You're doing fine." Compare that to what happens today. It's so different today that it barely seems like we're even the same species as the quaint people in that Toccoa church.

Growing up in the Bible Belt can lead a young girl into a confusing place with regard to medicine. I recall one time when I badly cut the arch of my right foot while playing in the back yard in Toccoa. It bled profusely. I was scared and didn't want anyone to know what had happened, so I ran to the side porch, propped my foot up on the porch rail and devoutly and earnestly prayed for a miracle. Around the time I figured out that my "instant healing" prayer hadn't been answered, my mother found me and discovered what had happened. She immediately called Dr. Ayers, who employed more medical knowledge in sewing my foot up than he routinely did with women who were expecting. I still carry the scar on my foot.

If my father hadn't lost his arm in that horrific ginning incident, his life, and in turn my own life, would have been far different. I suppose one could say that I was afforded the chance to be both the city mouse and the country mouse. We moved from hotel to hotel, following my father's acute business instincts, packing up our few belongings, our hopes, and our plans whenever my father sensed a new opportunity on the horizon, but we still managed to retain our stable, country roots in the northeastern corner of the thirteenth state.

I grew up in hotels around the South. Meeting new people each and every day, eating my daily meals in a hotel dining room, ringing that little silver front desk bell, watching the black bellmen scurry around carrying travelers' luggage to their rooms, learning how to operate the hotel telephone system, talking to strangers about their lives in far-flung places. These were simply normal, everyday aspects of my childhood, which I will happily describe with a tad more detail in the next chapter.

We always went to church, 11 o'clock service, wherever we were living, every Sunday. The first thing I really remember about a church service was being a part of the children's choir at De

Funiak Springs, Florida. We would march down the aisle during the processionals, feeling very important in our robes. I think it is most important for children to have a role in church services. In Toccoa, GA, where I spent the summers with my grandparents and aunts – Taudie and Teal – I remember attending all of the Vacation Bible Schools: Methodist, Baptist, Presbyterian...and having such fun. Singing the songs in Assembly, the cutting and coloring of pictures and the sampling of refreshments were all activities that I enjoyed immensely.

My aunts, Taudie and Teal, along with my mother, being raised washed in the life of the church, were essentially their own traveling choir. Their musical ability was beyond question. Aunt Emma, the oldest sister, was a talented organist, who sometimes accompanied the three singing Dimons. Their voices all had a different range: Mother was a soprano, Teal sang alto, and Taudie was a tenor. When you put the three of them together, their harmony would raise the holiness level of a church service up a tad.

Sunday afternoons we would sometimes "go to ride." I recall being in the car with Fred Northcutt, a family friend, driving, and just praying we would stop by the drugstore to get an ice cream cone (which cost 5 cents at the time).

I attended high school during World War II. The war-time home front was unlike any other time in American history. We came together as a nation. We took over the jobs normally performed by our soldiers. The country came together in this period in a way it never had previously. Soldiers from such seemingly exotic locales, like Brooklyn, San Francisco, and Anchorage, Alaska, would meet and bond, thrown together by incredible circumstance. Many of them would stay in one of our hotels. Dates were plentiful. It was a wondrous time to grow up.

Much later, I married and moved to Habersham County, where my husband was President of Habersham Mills. We'll get to that in the second half of the book.

My Early Years On The Move:
Georgia, Tennessee, Florida, Then Back To Georgia

Grandparents always have magical houses.

The house in Toccoa where my grandparents lived was built high off the ground in the back, sloping forward to ground level in the front, evening out the floor. As children, we would stand up under the house in the back and mark off the rooms above in the dirt below. Furniture, stoves, appliances, and bathrooms were make-believe with rocks and sticks piled up. It all made perfect sense to us. One of the "treasures" was a miniature iron stove. We made thousands of mud pies and baked them. I can also remember crawling under the house, toward the front, and out, under the front steps, as if I'd done it just yesterday. Memory is funny in that way.

~·~

In the evenings, we would run and catch lightning bugs, putting them in glass jars. Sometimes Teal would help us make candle cars, thin tissue paper contraptions into which we would place candles, before pulling them along the sidewalk with a string. These were the days when families sat out on the porch, or in the yard, in the summertime, and the children would play until bedtime.

~·~

This sounds crazy, but I don't remember ever being "disciplined." My mother didn't believe in corporal punishment, and I never remember being struck. I was never "taught" love. I was surrounded by it: parents, grandparents, and aunts.

⁓

In the hotels, the play was quite different. I can remember flying kites from the roof of the Holman Hotel in Athens, Georgia. Along with most of the rest of my generation, attending the picture show was my primary form of entertainment. The Saturday matinees lasted all afternoon at the old Strand, next to the Holman Hotel--a couple of cartoons, the next thrilling chapter of Flash Gordon or Lash Larue and a Western: Gene Autry, Hopalong Cassidy, etc. I saw more shows at The Strand, though it was generally thought that the best picture shows were inspiring other local children across the street at the Georgian Theater.

My hotel childhood was unique, but I didn't realize that then. I was awakened every morning with a wake-up call from the front desk operator saying, "Kathryn, it's 7:30. Time to get up." After dressing and making myself ready for the day, I took the elevator to the first floor for breakfast in the Dining Room, where I was served at a back table by a uniformed waitress. If the weather was inclement, I was driven to school by a bellman. If not, I walked. When I returned home after school around 3 P.M. Mother was there. This childhood freedom made me an independent woman well before the American feminist movement popularized the concept.

I did eat dinner with my parents. I talked about my day like any other child, though my dining room surroundings were a lot grander, and there were usually strangers at the next table. Naturally, I had relationships, close relationships, with many of Daddy's hotel employees. When Mother and Daddy were out of town, the hotel hostess, Allie Shaw, acted as my parent, in the Georgian Hotel.

I didn't have chores. I certainly never learned how to perform domestic duties. A colored maid made my bed. A series of talented chefs prepared all my meals. Some hotel staffer or another washed my clothes.

Although it is a rarer occurrence in hotels today, back then there were always a few "long-time residents," people who essentially lived in the hotel. I especially recall Moina Belle Michael. When American soldiers entered World War I, Moina Belle Michael, was a school teacher who lived in Athens. She knew she had to contribute. Some of the soldiers were her students and friends. Almost single-handedly, Moina worked to establish the red poppy as the symbol to honor and remember soldiers. And she devoted the rest of her life to making sure the symbol would last forever. She lived in the Georgian Hotel later in her life. I called her "The Poppy Lady". These residents, my childhood neighbors, sometimes played the part of baby-sitters, but they weren't substitute parents. Though both of my parents were loving and attentive, and though we were always surrounded by other people, we lived in our own little world, a world where, to an extent, I raised myself. In the years since I have found myself extremely grateful for the independent spirit my unique childhood circumstances conferred on me.

My brother Alwyn, being 9 years my senior, generally considered me a pest. And I must have been to him. I was really raised as an only child, always staying with my parents and he with my grandmother and aunts in Toccoa.

We lived in Murfreesboro, Tennessee when I was in first grade. Daddy had recently opened up the James K. Polk Hotel, a community-built project, meaning that the town leaders got together, raised the funds and actually built the hotel, hoping to use it to draw in tourists. Once it was constructed, Murfreesboro still needed someone who knew how to manage and run hotels. That's where my family came in. The Stiles Company (the name of the hotel management group my Daddy had formed with his two brothers) had signed a lease to run it. It was a good while ago and, honestly, my only remaining memory of my time in that middle Tennessee town was playing the triangle and "keeping time" in the children's rhythm group. It's a happy memory, but I wish I could recall more from that time.

I may not remember much from Murfreesboro, but I have a

treasure trove of memories from our next location. After Tennessee, we moved to De Funiak Springs, Florida. That was where I first met and got acquainted with the ocean, the Gulf of Mexico being just thirty miles south. Daddy had just opened The New Walton Hotel. The first time a child sees the ocean is always a memorable experience. However, De Funiak Springs meant so much more to me. That was where I met my first boyfriend. I can vividly look back on that boy giving me a ride home from school to the hotel on his bicycle. That's a big deal when you're a young girl.

I continued to be active in music in Florida, expanding my triangle playing mastery to include singing, joining the Methodist Church Children's Choir. I loved that choir. We had surplus choir robes (which I loved). We got to march down the aisle singing our hymns (which I loved). We were able to ease into religious life through pride and pageantry. NOTE TO MINISTERS---Involve the children early. You'll be glad you did.

De Funiak Springs also provided the young me with another common coming-of-age 20th century American childhood ritual... my first pair of roller skates. The town built an outdoor roller rink while we were there, and everyone in the area, including me, immediately went out and bought a pair of skates. Of course, I quickly experienced my first skating injury. I had a bad fall and cut a nasty gash under my chin, which was then clamped together rather than sewn. I've <u>never</u> been athletic.

It was back to The Baldwin Hotel in Milledgeville, Georgia for Junior High School. As a hotel child, you never stay in one place for very long, but it was comforting to have a place to bounce back to whenever we were between projects. For the Stiles family that place was The Baldwin Hotel in Milledgeville. Every semi-nomadic family needs a familiar place to recharge.

It helped that my grandparents, John Barrington Stiles and Mollie Lyle Allen Stiles, lived nearby, very nearby, in fact IN an apartment in the Baldwin Hotel. Grandpa was always good for a nickel. Like the bicycle boyfriend and the roller skates, the coin-dispensing grandfather is a big deal when you're a child. These events shape peoples' futures and affect their lives in ways not always seen until many years later.

My social life improved by leaps and bounds in that former state capitol. I met my second boyfriend in Milledgeville. G.M.C. (Georgia Military College) cadets were very much in evidence in that town. They were everywhere. We'd invite the cadets to our dances and our Friday night Prom Parties. This second boy took me to a "picture show" one Saturday afternoon, where I wore my first pair of heels. We'd host parties in Judge Carpenter's home with 6-8 girls and 6-8 cadets and play "Spin the Bottle." Judge Carpenter had two daughters around my age. I supposed that Milledgeville might be a place where we'd settled down, at least for a little while. I was wrong.

I could not have predicted that my parents would fall in love with Athens, Georgia. The next check-in chapter of my early life began when my father signed a lease on the magnificent Holman Hotel in Athens, on Clayton Street, the tallest building in Athens (then AND now—though after our time it was converted to a bank/office building). That building meant something to me. It was a part of my life, our lives, possibly even more so than the previous hotel/homes.

⁓⁓

The Holman Hotel was sold as a part of the Holman estate. Once again we moved temporarily to the Baldwin Hotel in Milledgeville. Subsequently Daddy bought the Georgian Hotel in Athens, so we moved back to Athens.

⁓⁓

High school is a life-changing experience for everyone. When you set that on top of the background of the American home front of World War II, trust me, it makes the memory so vivid, so iconically American, that it feels as much like a Jimmy Stewart movie as it does a memory.

I attended the Normal School on Oglethorpe and Prince Avenues. As one of the four lucky graduation speakers I recall my rousing, possibly naively far-fetched, but beautifully optimistic, speech about "Re-Educating the Nazi." It's good, and oh so

common, to know everything by age 16. Still, it was a good speech.
First, I've got to tell you about high school.

COMING OF AGE RIGHT ALONG
WITH THE ENTIRE COUNTRY

EVERYTHING WE DID IN HIGH SCHOOL LOOPED BACK TO WORLD War II somehow. It makes sense when you think about it. America came together as never before in World War II. The men and older boys were all overseas. Someone had to fill their shoes and perform their jobs, back in the good old U.S.A. Around here, those someones were us.

We sold war bonds and stamps. And, even more memorably, one day we made cotton picking into a game. I was pretty bad at it myself, but the mere fact that I can remember, this far removed, that Mavis Franklin, a sophomore at the time, was the Athens High School champion cotton picker, demonstrates how central the war was to our experience back then. Mavis picked 182 pounds of cotton in one day. That's a lot of cotton. She even beat the best male cotton picker by 47 pounds. But Athens, even then, was more of a university town than an agricultural one.

Personally, my biggest concern around that time was for my brother, Alwyn Stiles, who was a part of General George Patton's famed 2nd Armored Division. Most of us on the home front had relatives overseas, fighting for our country, waging war against fascism. We were proud of them, of course, but mainly we were scared for their lives. It was a war, after all, and people die in wars, the good and the bad alike.

Of course, even with a war on, I was still in high school. It's still high school, no matter where and when it is. I still did a lot of the things that high school kids do. I was active in The Beta Club and helped put together the annual. I was also in The Knit-Wits, a female social club. Due to my high marks, I was in the Honor Society. I had a role in the senior class play, "June Mad." As a superlative, I was even voted "Most Sincere" by my classmates. Perhaps the honor for which I am most proud, though, is that I was the Business Manager for the publication of the annual, selling ads to local businesses to pay for the publishing of our commemorative book. I was good at selling the ads, a skill that would come in handy for me later in life.

It wasn't all work for me, though. I did have an active social life. Gordon Statham and Danny Poss were my regular dates for social events like dances. Danny sent me my first orchid for the Junior-Senior Dance. Being in Athens meant that girls did not have to limit themselves to their male classmates for dates. There were college boys. There were Navy cadets. We had a lot of options.

Among other college boys, I specifically dated Olan Parr, a physics student at UGA. I feel the need to write a little about Olan. In the war Olan served with the Mountain Division of the ski troops of the U.S. Army, an assignment full of adventure if there ever was one. He won both the Purple Heart and the Bronze Star in combat and later built and worked on the first nuclear submarine. After the war Olan went on to become a Senior Executive with the United States Atomic Energy Commission. Olan was undoubtedly my first love.

As a woefully un-athletic sort, I was always picked last for every sporting event. It hurt a little at the time, but on the bright side, to this day I have had no broken bones in my body. How many people can say that at age 90?

Growing up in a hotel meant that my experience was unique in many ways. Rationing was enforced, of course. It was enforced everywhere. But as a hotel child, it didn't affect me nearly as much as it did everyone else. We did, however, cater to cadets. During the war years, the second floor of The Georgian Hotel was reserved for U.S. Army cadets in Army communication training, which in those days meant studying Morse Code. All hotels in the area were required to delegate a certain number of rooms for the military.

We lived on the top floor of the hotel. Just a few floors down was a large group of soldiers-in-training. My parents befriended the C.O. (Commanding Officer) of those cadets, and we had a number of pleasant social interactions with him. Like I said, the war was everywhere. That's why they called it a "World" war.

WHAT DO WE WANT? WHEN DO WE WANT IT?

I SHOULD SET THE SCENE A LITTLE. ATHENS HIGH SCHOOL WAS located in the old courthouse building. It wasn't your standard, era-appropriate one-room brick schoolhouse. We had large rooms with high ceilings. It was fairly cosmopolitan. For example, we were the only high school in the state which taught Latin (at the time). I still recall the first line of Julius Caesar's book, "Gaul as a whole is divided into three parts." We dissected frogs in biology class. Unlike many other high schools at the time we even had Spanish classes.

～･～

Everything was going swimmingly until the winter of our senior year was abruptly interrupted by A GENERAL STRIKE. Seriously, the students went on strike.

～･～

THE PLAN—Mr. E.B. Mell had been the Athens High School principal since its inception. He was beloved by the students, the teachers, and the town, which was inhabited by many of his former students, some of whom were leading figures in the community. The school board wanted to get rid of Mr. Mell under the auspices of a policy of "mandatory retirement." We students would have none of that. And so, we went on strike!

How many high school students can claim that they had so much school spirit, so much love for their principal, so much civic and national pride that they were willing to potentially jeopardize their futures by striking?

Of course, we planned the strike on the fifth floor of The Georgian Hotel. It was probably our most popular gathering place. Our senior class banquet was later held in the hotel ballroom. Not to brag too much, but, looking back, we participated in a well-planned strike. Longshoremen, teamsters, and auto workers could learn a thing or two about how to organize from us. We were able to not only flex our collective muscles through active non-participation, but to arouse the sympathy of the community. The graduates had overwhelmingly fond recollections of Mr. Mell, so we knew that we had public opinion on our side.

⚊⚬⚊

THE EXECUTION—We students gathered in the gymnasium. We all came to school...but not to learn. We came to make a point. Instead of entering the academic building, as we would've done on any other normal day, we stayed in the gym. Mandatory retirement?!? Why would someone who was great at his job, had the support of his underlings, his charges, and his city be forced to retire? It's not as if being a high school principal is manual labor. It's an intellectual job. It's a job that requires the patience that comes only with age.

Some kids stayed at the gym all day. Others of us went home or went and did other things. None of us went to class. The school board eventually yielded to our demand, and Mr. Mell wound up staying on until after our graduation.

Mr. Mell later attended my wedding. That's the kind of love we all had for our principal.

SUMMERING IN A BEAUTIFUL, BUT ISOLATED, APPALACHIAN MOUNTAIN HOTEL

AS MANY SOUTHERN FLAT-LANDERS DID IN THOSE DAYS, WEARY of the exhaustion brought on by the sweltering Southern summer heat made infinitely less bearable by the lack of air-conditioning, my family spent our summers in the North Carolina mountains. Unlike many other families, however, we had to work, but the temperature was still more tolerable. My father managed The Balsam Mountain Springs Hotel, a sprawling, three-story structure built in the 1800s in the "town" of Balsam. There was a railroad which ran through town, but not much more. Balsam was the highest elevation of any railroad stop east of the Rockies. The railroad and The Balsam Mountain Springs Hotel isolation gave the setting a magical feeling.

The first two stories of the hotel were set up for guests, while the help and staff lived on the third floor, along with us. This was due to the isolation. There was nowhere else for staffers to stay in Balsam. In fact, we had to import most of the staff. In our other hotels, we usually found workers in the community, but there was no community in the mountains to speak of. Consequently, most of our young, mostly female, wait staff was imported from a children's home in Atlanta of which my father was a trustee. We also hired reliable staffers from the other hotels, like Henry, the chef, a talented light-skinned black man from one of our other hotels. Because it takes a village to run a hotel, we often had to do much of the work ourselves. My Aunt Lucille Dimon ("Teal") made the salads. My mother was the entertainment. She looked beautiful and elegant as she played the piano in the lobby, pounding out hymns and popular standards of the time, putting her studies at Brenau College in "Piano" and "Voice" to good use entertaining the guests. My brother Alwyn cut the grass and was the general chauffeur for shopping and picnicking. We all contributed in our own way.

Like I said, we were catering to the people who came to escape the blistering Southern summer heat. That feeling of escape, coupled with the isolation and the beauty of the landscape created a kind of Shangri-La feeling. The excitement was palpable. Even the bridge tournaments were fun. I also vividly remember learning how to square dance at the Dance Pavilion on the hotel grounds, halfway down the mountain. The various communities (the industry groups and the multi-family vacationers) would each have their night of square dancing. I grew to really enjoy square dancing. There was always a string band, always a dance "caller."

Bear in mind, as well, that this was an era before television became the world's primary mode of entertainment. TV has its positive qualities, but it has surely separated us from one another. Our Balsam Mountain retreat created a sense of community in a way that is difficult to even describe to those who have grown up in this largely-impersonal Digital Age.

TURNING DOWN METHODIST SHEETS

THE STILES FAMILY'S NEXT DESTINATION WAS LAKE JUNALUSKA, North Carolina, an area known around the South as the premier Methodist summer retreat. While we were still in Balsam, Bishop Arthur Moore, a leading figure in the Methodist hierarchy, came to my father and asked him if he would take over the management of The Mission Inn in Lake Junaluska, which he did.

There were changes that needed to be made to The Mission Inn, so we made them. The church changed the name of the inn to The Lambuth Inn. Daddy delegated the running of the new inn to my Aunt Lillian Stiles Seville. Aunt Lillian was as talented and as hardworking as any of her brothers.

As an aside, I remember working the desk at The Lambuth Inn when I happened to check a kindly man in. He told me that he was the chaplain for the Second Armored Division, which naturally excited me, seeing as my brother Alwyn was himself a captain with that renowned division. And so, I made plans to talk with the chaplain, hoping to learn about what my brother was experiencing overseas. I was understandably excited and looked forward to hearing some detailed information from this first-hand source. The young people of today, readily communicating over the Internet even with relatives in far-flung wars may never have seen a redacted war-zone-to-home-front correspondence, but those were some of the least informative letters ever written. It was comforting to hear from them, however. Since the vast majority of what the soldiers would've written was considered classified, we were lucky to get a "Love, Alwyn" in readable print. This fact only served to make me more excited to talk to this supposed man of God. And then, to my dismay, when I did sit down with him, the chaplain took advantage of my tender age and my excitement, using it as an excuse to get a little too handsy. In retrospect, I'm not sure how holy he was.

We loved Lake Junaluska. Though it's known primarily as a summer retreat for regional Methodists, there was a community who lived there year-round. I can recall the many bicycles roaming the picturesque rolling hills, the giant lighted cross atop the hillside, and the huge playground. Daddy even bought a two-story lakeside home later, once his health began to decline. Having only one arm, he did, by that point, require some help in getting around and performing daily activities. He split his time during his golden years between Athens, Georgia (in the winters) and Lake Junaluska (in the summers).

Going Once…Going Twice…
Sold to the Well-Dressed, Boisterous,
One-Armed Gentlemanin the First Row

My father's hobby dovetailed nicely with his line of work. He loved going to art and jewelry auctions in Waynesville, NC. He loved the rush, the excitement, the thrill of the chase, the unbridled yet controlled frenzy of the environment. Auctions are capitalism at its finest. Anything can happen, and it's going to happen fast.

The auctioneers loved it when Daddy entered the room. His energy, enthusiasm and spirit of fun swept through the crowd and made an already-exciting event just a dash more thrilling. He was loud. He bid often. Daddy would often come back to Junaluska carrying a medical bag he used to carry the jewelry he had purchased.

By the time I knew what was happening, he'd long since caught the auction bug. What began as a means of procuring affordable and exotic hotel furnishings soon turned into his hobby, possibly the most expensive hobby he could have chosen. I recall Sheffield silver plates, large ornate candelabras, sterling silver tea services, Oriental rugs and more jewelry than I can name in one book. Daddy gave me a two-diamond platinum ring and later he gave me a 5-carat yellow canary diamond ring. He bid on so much jewelry that sometimes it would just fall out of his pocket. I remember once Teal was vacuuming and swept up a diamond ring. When she showed it to daddy he said, "Just keep it."

It wasn't just about what he could possibly bid on and buy at auction that lured my father to these happenings. It was the excitement in the air, the rush of the room when the frenzied bidding started. He was a part of it. If Daddy felt that things weren't moving fast enough, he'd just yell, "Sell It!!" More often than not, they'd do what he said. They'd sell it.

Daddy purchased many of our family treasures at those auctions.

John Stiles: Benign Autocrat

Daddy really was an autocrat. He gave orders and people followed them. They usually discovered that he had a plan in mind. He wasn't cruel or unnecessarily overbearing, but there was no doubt that he was the man in charge. From the perspective of my young and awed eyes, as long as Daddy was around, everything was taken care of.

When a man was out of work, Daddy found him a job. My father felt responsible to the community (and to the family), no matter which community we had moved into at the time. He was successful and believed deeply in the maxim: "With great privilege comes great responsibility."

That's not to say that Daddy supported laziness in any form. He was a hard-worker, and so he demanded hard work from everyone around him. He was not a hands-on type of parent, never traditionally affectionate. Daddy was affectionate in his own way, but he was never a "cuddly" father.

I don't mean to imply that there wasn't love in our family. There was abundant love. We were surrounded by love. Despite his austerity, Daddy was generous to a fault, and my Mother was quite loving. When I got sick, she was always there with chicken or beef broth, a warm cloth for my chest, and Vicks Vap-O-Rub. She was a big believer in the healing power of Vicks and milktoast. Mother was a bit of a worrier.

After one long illness I was fed eggnog: a rich concoction of whipped cream and raw eggs, laced with whiskey (a Southern cure if there ever was one). Since I was a thin child, Mother worked hard to put meat on my bones, a constant frustration for my caring, worrisome Mother. I suffered from tonsillitis often as a youth, but Mother refused to let the doctor take out my tonsils. Aunt Etta, my father's sister, had bled to death having hers removed, and that thought scared Mother away from that idea for good.

ON MY OWN...SORT OF

AFTER HIGH SCHOOL I WAS PACKED AWAY TO THE WARD Belmont School for Girls, a "finishing school" in Nashville, Tennessee where I would spend one grueling year of my young life. They were unbelievably strict about everything at Ward Belmont. We were not allowed to wear pants. We were not allowed to wear shorts. We HAD to wear panty hose, sensible heels, smart skirts, and conservative blouses...all day...every day. It was a finishing school that I desperately wanted to be finished with.

Looking back now, I'm sure my Mother had a hand in the decision to ship me off to Ward Belmont. She was afraid that my active social life would wind up "getting me in trouble," to use the parlance of the times.

Finishing schools hovered somewhere in between high schools and colleges. Like high schools, there were strict and plainly-set-out rules which <u>had</u> to be obeyed. Like colleges, we lived in tightly-packed dormitories with hundreds of other girls of the same age. Like high schools, we were naïve young women struggling to puzzle out the big questions of life. Like colleges, we roamed the campus, traveling to the Academic Building for classes and back to the dorms for study and free time (not that there *was* much free time).

If you were to ask one of the school marm-ish administrators of Ward Belmont why they were so strict, she likely would have told you that their guidelines existed to "mold girls into proper young ladies" or some such blather. Many of my classmates were raised in privilege. They were the daughters of rich and powerful families, whose parents thought they needed some mental and moral tweaking, a wash and wax job on their social graces, before being released into the wild world...on their own...for the first time.

We had almost no social life at The Ward Belmont School for Girls. So far as I was concerned, it was Dullsville. I didn't feel like I was anything there, merely existing, uninterested in anything other than discovering the date of my departure. I'm sure that actual prison inmates feel much the same. At the time I didn't think that I needed "finishing." I was ready to see what the world had in store for me. Luckily for me, I didn't have to wait very long, and was only forced to stay at Ward Belmont for one year. After that, I suppose I was "finished" enough.

AND NOW ON TO A REAL COLLEGE

AFTER SPENDING MY FRESHMAN YEAR AT THE WARD BELMONT School for Girls, I transferred to Wesleyan College in Macon, Georgia, for my sophomore and junior years. Wesleyan was a small Methodist college, the oldest and best girls' school around, located in the moderate-to-large sized city of Macon. There was so much more going on at Wesleyan than at Ward Belmont, and that was what this young lady wanted at the time. I got to live a little.

Quite a lot happened to me in college, as it often does to people at that age. I quickly met a woman who would become my roommate and later my friend-for-life, Margaret Parsons, from Duluth, Georgia. We bonded immediately and have remained close friends for the rest of our lives. Margaret was a brave soul. Years down the road, she contracted Parkinson's Disease and volunteered to be the first patient for a new surgery where the doctors literally sliced off the top of her head in order to probe different parts of her brain, all while she was still awake. She interacted with the doctors and answered their questions as the top of her skull was literally sitting on a metal tray next to her. That's bravery.

Seeing as I had been so cooped up at Ward Belmont, I enjoyed my newfound freedom at Wesleyan. That meant dates. Lots of dates. I have always had a strong attraction to men. Lieutenant

Bruce McArthur was stationed at Camp Wheeler. With *that* particular last name, he had to expect to spend some time in the military. John Belk, a member of the department store family of the same name, also took me out. I wasn't particularly interested in John, but he did have one thing going for him. He drove a convertible. Of course, we enjoyed the normal dating activities of that era, like going to the movies and "parking," but when we felt like dressing up and doing it right, the Dempsey Hotel dining room was the place to go for evening dates in Macon.

I studied various subjects at Wesleyan, but honestly, my favorite subject was dating. My interest in learning didn't come until years later. Travel would later become my window into the world, my true education, but that was still well down the road. Though I was on track to graduate in 1947, I dropped out to pursue an "MRS" degree (marriage) and wouldn't set foot back in the classroom until many years later under some strange circumstances. We'll get to that later.

I do cherish my time at Wesleyan and have set up an annuity payable to the school upon my passing from this world.

Meeting My Husband, Marion Stribling

I was visiting my two aunts in Mount Airy, Georgia when my life changed irrevocably for the better. The war was winding down and soldiers were returning home. That night there happened to be a dance at the community center in Cornelia, a slightly larger town just down the road from Mt. Airy. Calvin Stovall, recently returned from the war, had asked me to accompany him as his date to the dance.

As we were parking at the center, a car pulled up near us, parked right next to Calvin's, and a tall, lanky, 6'4" man confidently climbed out and said hello to Calvin. Calvin introduced me, "Oh, Kathryn, I want you to meet my life-long friend, Marion Stribling." Marion happened to have been driving through Cornelia and had seen the cars gathering at the community center, so he decided to see what the fuss was about.

I went to the dance that night with two very handsome, very eligible, ex-military bachelors. I wound up dancing with both of them and liked them both quite a bit. Marion managed to persuade me to give him my aunts' phone number, and he called me for a date the very next day. For a time I dated both of them, not being entirely privy to the behind-the-scenes details of the competition between these two good friends, a competition in which I was the prize.

I later learned about the following story. Calvin owned and operated the Ford Motor Company in Cornelia. One night, after I had been dating both Calvin and Marion for a time, Marion, seeing the light on in Calvin's office, pulled in and had a "serious talk" with him.

It went something like:

Marion—"I have plans to marry Kathryn Stiles."

Calvin—"Well, I plan to marry her, too, so it's going to be a little crowded."

They were such good friends that they followed the age-old tradition of both pursuing me and "letting the best man win." Marion was the best man. Despite the competition, he and Calvin stayed good friends. He even gave Marion his bachelor party and stood up with him at our wedding as a groomsman. Daddy was a little disappointed that I didn't marry Calvin, since it meant that he couldn't get good deals on Fords in the future. He was initially against the marriage, though not specifically against my marrying Marion, more generally against the idea of my getting married to anyone. I recall sitting in the Georgian Hotel when I told him, and I'll never forget his flat-out refusal to endorse it.

Me—"I'm going to marry Marion Stribling."

Dad—"No, you're not."

⁓⁓⁓

Those were his exact words. Though he had his qualms about his daughter marrying anyone, Daddy did end up liking and respecting Marion. They got along well from the start. He did, however, warn me that I would wind up a widow for a long time, seeing as Marion was twelve years my elder.

My wedding day, April 12th, 1947 was a beautiful spring day. We were living at 225 Hampton Court in Athens. As you could probably safely assume by now, my bridal preparations didn't go entirely as planned. When I was bathing, as bridal luck would have it, the hot water gave out and I wound up taking a cold bath on my wedding day!

Aunt Emmie played the organ and Bertha Motz played the violin. My sobering cold bath wasn't the only misstep of my wedding day. The florist forgot the petals for the flower girls, so they just tore up their head pieces and used those. I wore my sister-in-law, Catherine Wingate Stiles,' wedding dress. It was a lovely wedding, and the reception was held at the Georgian Hotel.

We didn't have much money at the time, so we honeymooned right down the road (the very long road) in Savannah Beach. Mrs. Earl Knight, a silent partner of Daddy's in the hotel business, lent us the keys to her Savannah Beach cottage for a honeymoon. It was wonderful.

Honeymoon expenses, 1949

breakfast (Ozzie's Eatery)	$1.45
hotel (Eatonton)	10.00
gas (Milledgeville)	2.20
drinks (Waynesboro)	.10
lunch (Aid's Barbecue Savannah)	1.05
Delicatessen	1.57
lunch (DeSota)	3.30
gift (Mrs. Knight)	5.00
groceries (Tybee Market)	1.58
T.S. Chu 5&10 (powder puff, comb, frying pan, bathing trunks)	5.69
postal cards & stamps	.20
	$32.14
dinner (Johnny Harris')	$6.00
gas (Cities Service Golden Rule)	3.10
Hotel (DeSota)	6.10
newspaper	.05
lunch	3.25
dinner	4.00
lunch	3.25
bookends	5.00
	30.75
	32.14
	$62.89
lunch	1.16
gas (Statesboro)	2.35
telephone & telegram	.74
gas (Athens)	3.60
	$12.75
	62.89
	$75.64

HABERSHAM COUNTY:
MILL LIVING IS A WHOLE DIFFERENT WORLD

RETURNING "HOME" FROM OUR SAVANNAH BEACH HONEYMOON, I didn't just settle in with Marion in our newly-painted home, I moved into a place that was a completely different world from the hotel life I had been accustomed to. It felt as if I had been transported to a new planet, with new rules, new people, new etiquette, even a new time. Hotel time is different from Habersham County mill time. I'd never gotten up with the chickens before. I'd never even cooked a meal before. Even boiling water, the simplest task in the cooking handbook, was totally foreign to me!

Fortunately, I quickly learned one of the positive realities of mill life. There's always a helpful neighbor around somewhere close by. We moved into a house right next door to my mother-in-law, who would become my chief tour guide through the twists and turns of this odd new reality I found myself in. Not only was I "in" farm life, by virtue of my new husband's elevated position of superintendent of the mill, I had become the model of a modern miller's wife. I needed to learn how to boil water--and fast.

HABERSHAM TIME:
BEFORE STRIBLINGS

JUST AS YOU ENTER THE MILL VILLAGE THERE IS AN HISTORICAL marker proudly stating that this land was the earliest location north of Augusta to be used as an industrial site in the state of Georgia. Like most historical markers, it's true though incomplete. In other words, a lot happened in Habersham even before the Striblings came on the scene.

⁓⌘⁓

Habersham County has been mill land for the vast majority of the area's history. The awesome power of the Soque River was sitting there, ready to be harnessed by far-sighted industrious men. First a German immigrant named Stoub opened and operated an iron factory. He later left the area, moving to Birmingham, Alabama and opening an iron business in what would become a large industrial hub of the Southeast.

The founder's leaving opened the door for others to take the reins... and they did. The Habersham Iron Works and Manufacturing Company incorporated in 1837 under the leadership of Jarvis Van Buren, a cousin of America's 8th president, Martin Van Buren. Jarvis was a pioneering railroad man and an industrial wizard who arrived in the area when it was still largely Indian country. Oddly (considering that Jarvis was a railroad man and that his family connections were about as good as was humanly possible), the area didn't merit a rail-spur line, meaning that all supplies, all products produced, all imports and all exports, had to come to the region via mule train from Augusta. One of the stock holders for the Habersham Iron Works and Manufacturing Company was the famed Southern firebrand politician and former Vice President, John C. Calhoun. This industrial incarnation of the area only operated for a few years, shutting its doors for the moment. Its isolation was its downfall.

Although the Iron Works didn't last long, the machinery, the factory, and the abundant power supply were still around, waiting for the right moment to reopen the doors and turn the machines back on. That moment came in the 1860s during The War Between the States, when the Iron Works began making ammunition for the Confederacy. There were not many munitions plants in the South during the war. Some historians claim that this was ultimately the downfall of the Confederacy and, had the South industrialized instead of relying on Northern and European factories, the outcome of the war would have been altogether different.

Though the Confederacy lost the war, the output of the Iron Works proved that the area could function as a viable industrial center. In the 1880s, the Porter Manufacturing Company and Woolen Mills, more commonly known as Porter Mills, took control of the plant and changed the focus from munitions and farm equipment to processing the raw materials of the South, textiles and woolen garments. Porter Mills also did not last long, going bankrupt not long after it opened its doors. The site lay vacant for another twenty years or so...until S.Y. Stribling, Sr., got a notion.

OVER THE RIVER AND THROUGH THE HILLS

IN 1906 S.Y. STRIBLING SR. LAID EYES ON THE OLD PORTER MILLS site, dormant for a few decades, and thought that it would be ideal for the manufacture of cotton yarn. His prediction rang true, as the mill remained in operation under the Stribling banner for nearly a century. Like all great businesses, it started with an idea.

S.Y. came to the area from Roswell, Georgia, where he was the president of the Bank of Roswell and was associated with the textile mill in Roswell. Already an accomplished banker and businessman, his eye was well-trained to spot opportunity on the horizon. He knew the history of Porter Mills and of the Iron Works. He recognized the power of the Soque River and saw how it could be harnessed. Being a Southerner, he had heard the Civil War stories. All Georgia boys at that time grew up on tales of the "War of Northern Aggression" and knew them by heart. Those lost Utopian tales were second only to Bible stories for Southern boys born near the "turn of the century."

Arriving in Habersham County, knowing what could be, but not seeing anyone around to ask about it, S.Y. Sr., the Founding Father and first president of what was to become Habersham Mills, needed some information from a local. Unfortunately, he couldn't *find* any locals. Migration patterns tend to follow economic development. The mill had been abandoned for a generation, and so nobody was around. There was, however, a giant bell tower on top of the mill building. Being an enterprising man, S.Y. Sr. climbed the stairs outside of the factory, surveying the state of the machinery, and, when he reached the tower, rang the bell as hard as he could. He kept ringing it until someone noticed. Eventually, a curious watchman came by, S.Y. climbed down, and they talked. There was nobody around and he wouldn't have even discovered that watchman if he hadn't had the initiative to climb up the tower and ring that bell.

S.Y. Sr. then set about rebuilding the mill, starting the production back up again, converting it to handle textile manufacturing, and repurposing it to fit his and Georgia's needs servicing King Cotton. Being a banker, he knew how to raise capital, which was fortunate because he needed to finance the project. Being an industrialist familiar with the textile operations in Roswell, he knew how to develop industry, which was equally fortunate because he needed to construct an entirely new mill. He saw his opportunity, and he took it.

Marion Stribling arrived in Habersham County *en utero*. If his father hadn't received a call from T. Earle Stribling (S.Y. Sr.'s son and the president of the mill at the time) asking him to come to Habersham from Roswell to build that second hydro-electric plant, the chain of events that led to my five children wouldn't have happened. It has always amazed me how one single happening can change the course of an entire generation, one event that seems so minor at the time can alter and shape whole lives, which then go on to alter more lives, and so on.

S.Y. Stribling Jr.'s and his pregnant wife, Kite's, and their oldest child, S.Y. III's first glimpses of their future home was a rural railroad whistle stop. The three then climbed into a wagon for the 4-mile trip to The Village. By the time the construction of the "lower power plant" ended, as it was known by the locals, S.Y. Jr. and Kite, S.Y III. and Marion had settled into the area. It had become home.

⌒⌒⌒⌒

Though it is rural, the Habersham area has been a pioneer on many fronts. We had electricity before there was such an entity as Georgia Power. There was a river. There was a mill. There was gravity. Therefore, we generated power using the means at our disposal, the steady but raging flow of the Soque River. In fact, we produced so much power that we had enough left over to sell energy to Clarkesville before the REA (FDR's New Deal program for providing electricity to rural America) reached our doors.

It was this power that allowed Habersham Mills to turn baled cotton into long cotton yarn. That's what we did, taking the labor of the King Cotton South and changing it into a useful form, to be shipped to clothing manufacturers, bedding outlets, and other industries who wanted Georgia cotton for their products. The South has historically grown a lot of cotton, so there was always work for the mill and a good living for its employees.

The employees worked hard at the mill, but it wasn't ALL work. They played, too. Far and away the favorite pastime in Habersham was also America's favorite pastime, baseball. Back then textile mills would often field their own baseball teams, competing for pride and bragging rights against other mills' teams. There might have been some side bets for actual money, too, but I wasn't privy to that. Mainly, it was just fun. Clarkesville Mill, Gainesville Mill and even a few teams over the South Carolina border were our main competition.

Marion was an excellent athlete. He'd lettered in baseball and basketball at Clemson, and his skills hadn't diminished by the time we married. He was a good batter and always played first base. He was an impressive sportsman in other sports, too, always involved in outdoor sports, like hunting and fishing. Baseball is a rural game. Look at the backgrounds of most major league baseball players and you're going to discover that most of them grew up in the country. Country boys are tough. Marion fractured an arm five times during baseball games. He was always running into other players, determined to stretch a single into a double. He was good, so he often hit doubles, but he also often wound up running into a lot of people. Marion was so good that he was later elected to The Textile Baseball Hall of Fame.

The mill baseball games were a big deal. I had never seen a baseball game until I moved to Habersham. Everyone in the village came out, grabbed a seat in the grandstands, packed some snacks, and lugged the children along to cheer for the home team, especially seeing as the home team was comprised of their fathers. We were very isolated, and so these games were the social events of the region. Baseball was an area of Habersham life where the social classes freely mixed and mingled. If the janitor was a better center fielder than the president, then he was the guy playing in center field. Those guys played to win. A good baseball player would always stand a better chance of being hired as an employee in the mill.

Second to baseball, fishing was probably the most popular pastime in Habersham. We had a well-stocked lake. Everybody had a fishing boat. We ate a lot of fish. Not surprisingly, I learned early on how to cook fish.

The mill was always looking for ways to improve the village social life. Eventually, they built an Olympic-size swimming pool and bath house next to the lake for the enjoyment of all. This was a big deal. We had four lanes. We had a diving board. The Georgia summers can be brutal and there's nothing like taking a dip in a real pool to cool off. We charged 10 cents for entry for mill employees.

Everyone else had to pay a quarter, and the funds went to pool upkeep and maintenance. All of my children took full advantage of our pool, becoming Red Cross certified lifeguards. The mill also built two tennis courts, but they were never popular. Everybody loved the pool, but trying to introduce country club sports to the region was a bit much. We might as well have built polo grounds for all the use the tennis courts got.

Due to my unique upbringing, my Habersham adjustment period lasted longer than most. I have plenty of examples in my memory banks. Most of them took place in "The Pasture," the large grassy area adjacent to our house. Mr. Stribling, Marion's father, would milk the cows each night. Living next door, it was a simple task for him to come over and relieve the cows each and every evening, around 5 P.M. Once, when he and Marion's mother were away on a trip, Marion dutifully took over the milking duties when he got home from work. Desiring to help and to learn, I volunteered to help and was assigned to pour off the strain and then dump the milk into bottles for later use. Marion had to suppress a laugh when I, in all seriousness, asked, "So, how do you separate the milk from the cream?" I quickly learned. I also figured out how to churn butter and perform other common domestic tasks, but I had my limits. I let the men raise and slaughter the pigs and hang them in the smokehouse.

As a self-contained village, Habersham naturally had a school. Though the kids were bused to nearby Clarkesville for high school, we had a functioning small, brick elementary school in the village, servicing first through seventh grades. The mill paid for the amenities, including an extra teacher in order to keep the class sizes small and ensure a reasonable teacher/student ratio. Figuring that our little school would be the sum total of most of the local children's educations, we did what we could to make it a better experience. The mill paid for the supplies. I essentially WAS the PTA, entirely by default, but I still managed to improve things a little. For example, after securing permission from the parents, I made sure that all of the kids received the Salk polio vaccine. By the time Zachary and Mary came on the scene, the school had closed and the mill children were attending school in Clarkesville. But our little mill elementary school had been far superior to any other school in the area.

The definitive book written about the mill, Edna Holcomb's *A Time That Was: The Habersham Mills Story* (Holcomb, Edna, All Service Printing, Clarkesville, GA, 2012), contains an accurate and personal description of the basic geography of the region, as told by local Stan Terrell. "The mill village consisted almost entirely of steep hills and very narrow valleys and hollows, or as most called

Joseph H. Gill Stiles
b. 1779
d. 2/15/1858

Joseph Eugene Stiles
b. 6/21/1819
d. 1898

John Barrington Stiles
b. 10/15/1860
d. 6/28/1947

John Campbell Stiles
b. 1/21/1894
d. 6/3/1974

Amanda Lane Yarbrough
b. 2/25/1817
d. 3/7/1890

Claudia Graves Yarbrough Dimon
b. 3/8/1857
d. 2/27/1935

Mary Haygood Dimon Stiles
b. 12/14/1890
d. 12/11/1979

Kathryn Haygood Stiles Stribling
b. 9/20/1926

John Stiles, 11 years, Etta Stiles, 9 years, Josie Stiles, Pearl Stiles, Sally Scoggins, Caro Gibson, Allen Stiles, Caro Green, Rowdy the cow

Back row: Allen Stiles, Sr, Johns Stiles, Clifford Stiles
Front Row: Pearl Stiles Green, Josie Stiles Harper, Lilian Stiles Saville

58

The Dimon sisters. Mary, Lucile (Teal), Taudie and Emma

John Barrington Stiles and his wife Mollie Allan Stiles

John Campbell Stiles and Mary Haygood Dimon Stiles

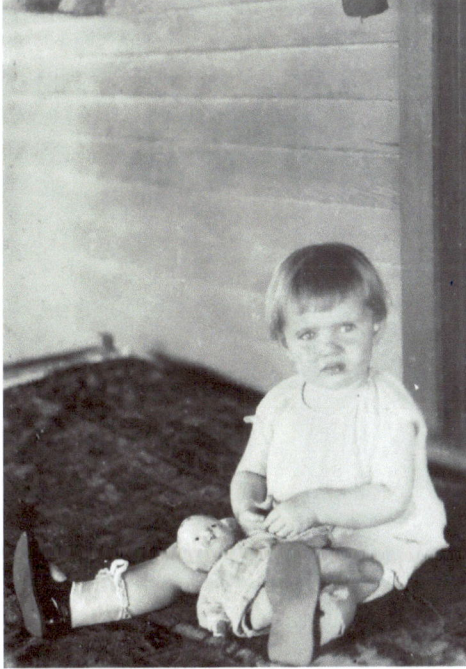

Kathryn and her doll around age 3

Mary Stiles, Kathryn and Alwyn

John and Mary Stiles, Alwyn and Kathryn

Kathryn Stiles Stribling

Mary Dimon Stiles and her daughter, Kathryn

Kathryn's high school graduation photo, 1943

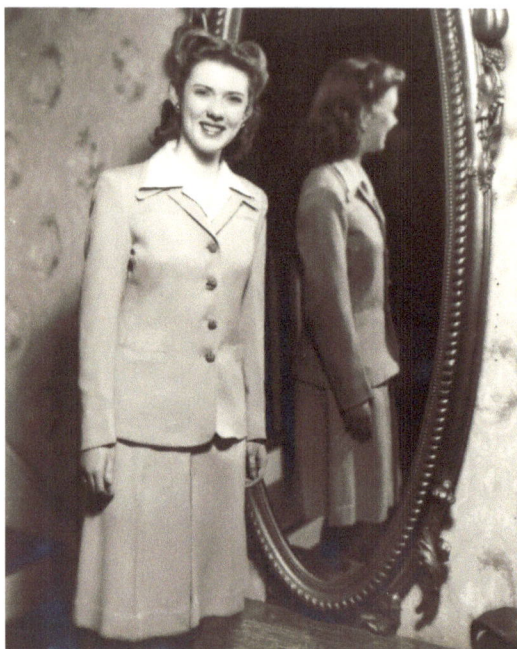

Kathryn Stiles, Ward Belmont, Nashville, TN

Alwyn Stiles, WWII

The Baldwin Hotel, Milledgeville, GA

The Baldwin Hotel, Milledgeville, GA

James K Polk Hotel, Murfreesboro, TN

James K Polk Hotel, Murfreesboro, TN

The New Walton Hotel, De Funiak Springs, Fla.

The New Walton Hotel, De Funiak Springs, FL

Holman Hotel, Athens, Ga.

The Holman Hotel, Athens, GA

Balsam Mountain Springs Hotel, Balsam, NC

Balsam Mountain Springs Hotel ad, Balsam, NC

Balsam Mountain Springs Hotel ad, Balsam, NC

Mission Building / Lambuth Inn, Lake Junaluska, NC

Mission Building / Lambuth Inn, Lake Junaluska, NC

Georgian Hotel, Athens, GA

Georgian Hotel, Athens, GA

1947 wedding photo of Marion and Kathryn Stribling

Kathryn, on her wedding day

Marion and Kathryn's wedding reception at the Georgian Hotel

Marion and Kathryn, John Stiles with John Winters Stribling, Mary Stiles

John Stiles' portrait hung in each of his hotels

John Stiles, holding a fish he caught in the Gulf of Mexico near Panama City, FL

Stribling Family Reunion, Green Grove Farm, Milledgeville, Georgia. Pictured are Mr. & Mrs. John C. and Mary Dimon Stiles and their children, Alwyn and Catherine Wingate Stiles and their children, Doreen, Jane, Lynn and Ann. Marion and Kathryn Stribling and their children, John, Jack and Sloan.

Children of Alwyn and Catherine Stiles and Marion and Kathryn Stribling (back row): Lynn, John, Doreen holding Mary, Ann, Sloan (front row): Jack, Zachary, Barry, Jane

The Marion Stribling Christmas Card, 1958

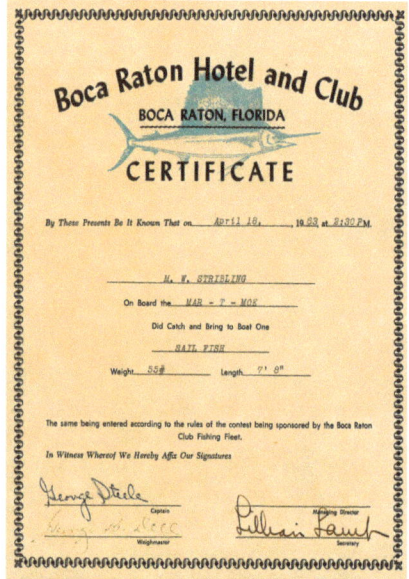

(Left) Kathryn poses with Marion and two sailfish she caught with Marion's help on vacation in Boca Raton, Florida on April 18, 1963. (Right) A certificate from the Boca Raton Hotel & Club acknowledging Marion's catch.

Portrait of Marion Winters Stribling

Display booth of Kathryn's work at the Habersham County Fair, August, 1979

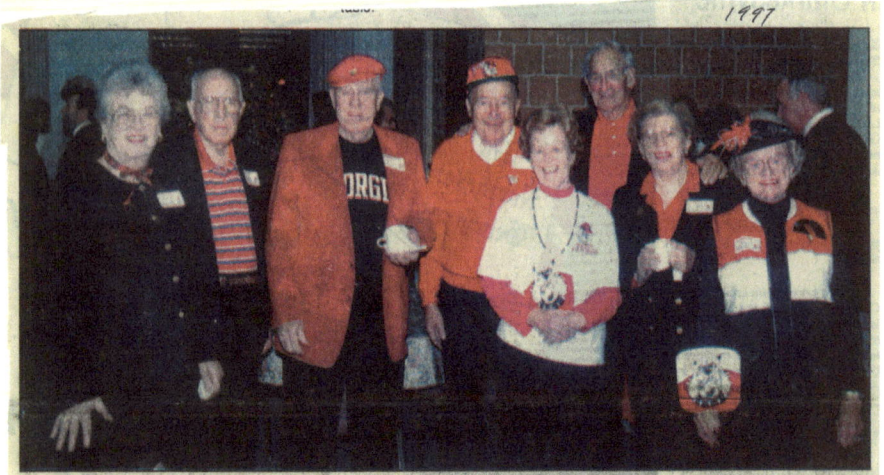

Edna Ellard, Jack Ellard, Calvin Stovall, Bill and Lois Shortt, Marion — red and black — during the Habersham County Chamber of Stribling, Kathryn Stribling and Nancy Stovall show off their true colors Commerce's annual membership meeting last week.

Our social group that met for dinner every Friday night for over 30 years

Marion and Kathryn's Friday Night group

Kathryn and Marion at a convention

Kathryn and Marion - 50th wedding anniversary

Alwyn and Kathryn at Lake Burton

Kathryn and her Great Grandchildren,
Parker, Annie and Kite.

Kathryn Stiles and her progeny on the front lawn of the old Stribling house, Roswell, Georgia

(left to right): Jack, Jason, John and Parker Stribling (young boy) at the house of Jonathan and Jessica Stribling in Demorest, Georgia, Thanksgiving, 2012

Kathryn's Travels...

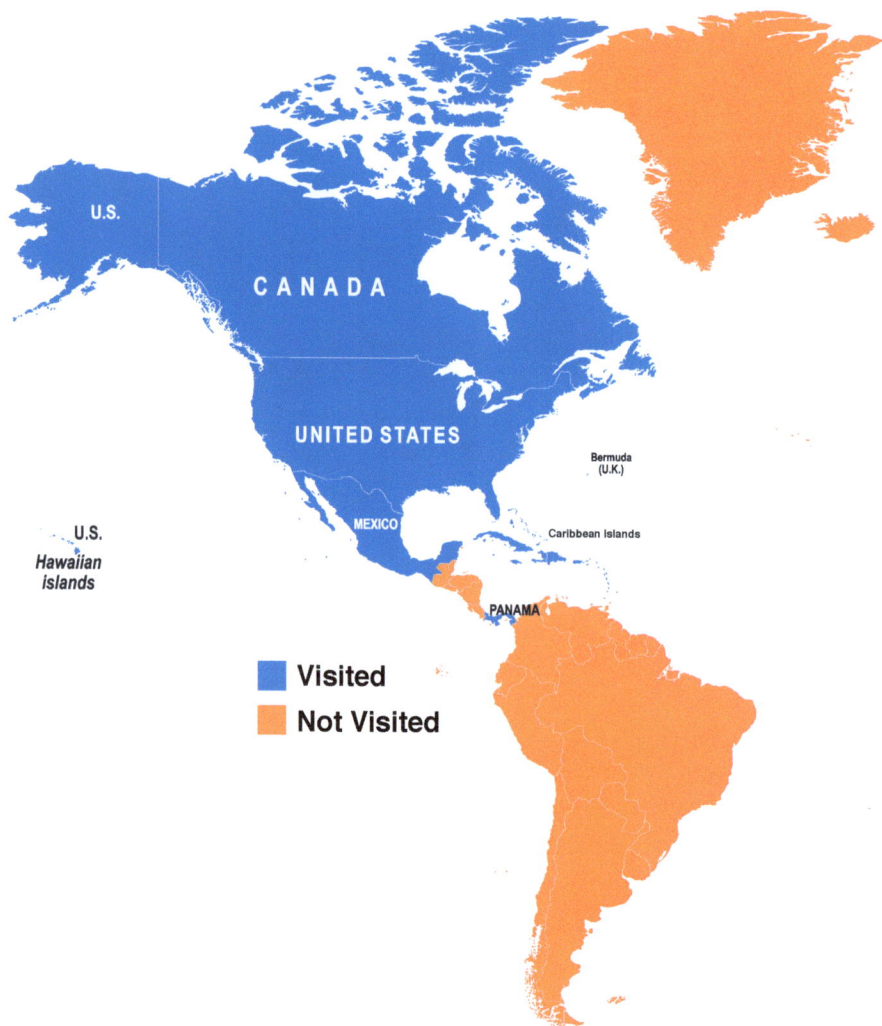

U.S.

CANADA

U.S.

UNITED STATES

Bermuda
(U.K.)

U.S.
*Hawaiian
islands*

MEXICO

Caribbean islands

PANAMA

Visited

Not Visited

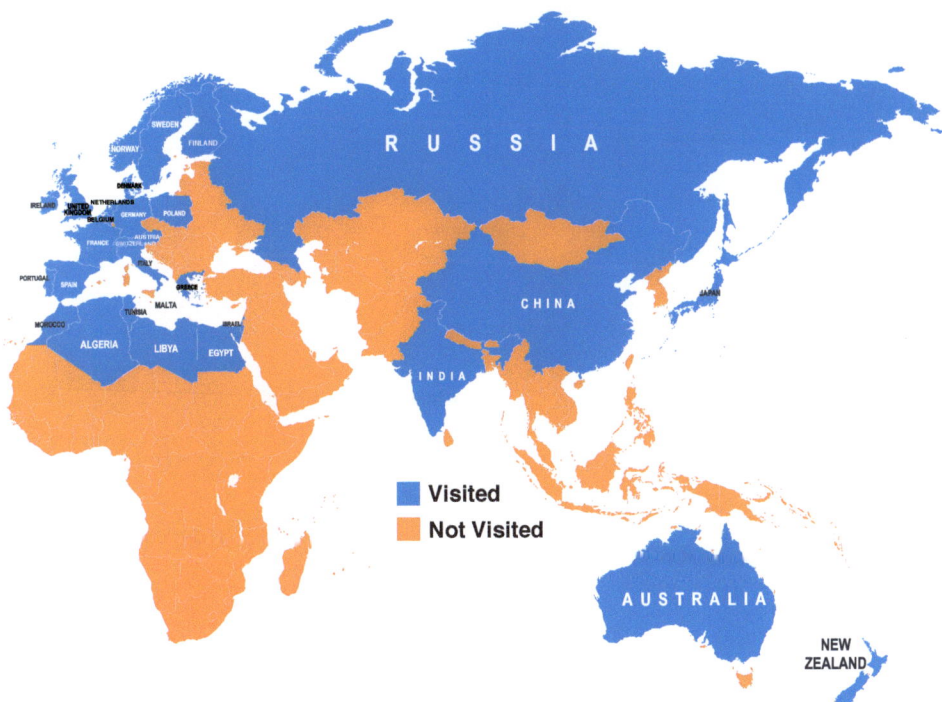

Nations visited...

Amsterdam	Germany	New Zealand
Australia	Great Britain	Norway
Austria	Greek Islands	Panama Canal
Belgium	India	Poland
Bermuda	Ireland	Portugal
Canada	Israel	Scotland
Casablanca	Italy	Spain
China	Japan	Sweden
Denmark	Mexico	Switzerland
Egypt	N. African Coast (all)	USSR
France	Netherlands	United States

Piedmont College

The Board of Trustees upon the recommendation of the Faculty
has conferred upon

Kathryn Stiles Stribling

the degree

Bachelor of Arts

with all the rights, honors and privileges thereunto appertaining
Witness the seal of the College and the signatures of its only
authorized officers hereto affixed
Given at Demorest, Georgia
June 2, 1968

President of the College

Chairman of the Board of Trustees

HCLC Pioneer Award

presented to

Kathryn Stribling

March 14, 2008

in appreciation of your vision and
perseverance in establishing

Habersham Christian Learning Center

"Train up a child in the way he should
go: and when he is old,
he will not depart from it."
Proverbs 22:6

Wesleyan College News

Volume XIX   Number 1   Winter 1990

Kathryn Stribling's Gift Ensures Wesleyan's Future

As a young girl, Kathryn Haygood Stiles Stribling '47 traveled around the state of Georgia with her parents as they attended various college trustee meetings. Her father, John Campbell Stiles, also participated in fund raising campaigns at Wesleyan. From these early childhood experiences, Mrs. Stribling started to establish her own set of priorities.

For Kathryn Stribling, an important aspect of growing up as a Methodist was to support Methodist colleges. "It was a part of my lifestyle," Mrs. Stribling said in a recent interview. "Support for colleges came from the family. It went along with my Methodist heritage," she added.

So, it was more or less natural, and inevitable, for her to make a gift to Wesleyan. On December 15, 1988, Kathryn Stribling transferred 3,111 shares of Kemper International, a mutual fund, to Wesleyan College. At the time of the transaction, the gift had a face value of $28,125.

Dinner Honors Charter Members in The Society for the Twenty-First Century

Among those attending a dinner to recognize charter members in The Society for the Twenty-First Century were (left to right) Addie Rie McKellar Baird '50, Pree Sell, and Mary Ann Peacock Powell '76.

The donation was given in memory of her father and qualified her as a member of the President's Council (gifts over $10,000) during the 1988-89 Annual Loyalty Fund drive. Since her gift was an annuity, it also qualified her as a charter member in The Society for the Twenty-First Century, a planned giving recognition program. Hers was the first gift annuity to Wesleyan during the college's new emphasis on planned giving. It has served as a model for others.

"For some time, I had intended to make Wesleyan a beneficiary of some funds one way or another," she said from her home in Habersham, GA. Mrs. Stribling was prompted to act following an alumnae meeting in Atlanta. Donald J. Welch, vice president for institutional advancement at Wesleyan, made a presentation explaining various giving plans, including gift annuities.

"I immediately saw this as the route to go," she said. "From a business point of view, it was advantageous."

Simply put, a gift annuity is more than just a gift. It is an investment for Mrs. Stribling and Wesleyan. She receives more income from her gift annuity than she did when her money was invested in a mutual fund. And she is "very happy" with the tax breaks.

Mrs. Stribling highly recommends giving plans. "It is good business from a tax standpoint and from a straight income standpoint," she said. "Not only do you help Wesleyan, but you also help yourself," she added.

The Stribling family has some Wesleyan ties. Kathryn Stiles Stribling attended Wesleyan for her sophomore and junior years, majoring in English with Dr. Gignilliat. She would have graduated with the class of '47 if she had not followed her heart and married. Mrs. Stribling graduated in 1967 from Piedmont College in Demorest, GA with her eldest son.

Kathryn Stiles Stribling

Her mother-in-law, Katherine Suddath Stribling '11, is the oldest living Wesleyan alumna. This May, she will celebrate her 101st birthday. Kathryn Stiles Stribling also had a great aunt, Mattie Haygood Ardis, who graduated from Wesleyan in 1888.

Methodist colleges and the Stribling family have a long history together. Her father was chairman emeritus of the board of trustees at Reinhardt College in Waleska, GA. In addition, he was on the trustee boards at Young Harris College in Young Harris, GA and LaGrange College in LaGrange, GA. Today, her husband, Marion Stribling, is a trustee at Young Harris College.

Strong Methodist beliefs and strong family ties to Methodist colleges guided Mrs. Stribling not only to attend Wesleyan College, but to help ensure Wesleyan's future as the school becomes the pre-eminent woman's college in the Southeast.

(Please turn to pages two and three for more information on The Society for the Twenty-First Century and gift annuities.)

Service of Dedication
Wednesday, June 22, 1955 — 5:15 P. M.
STILES-DIMON CHAPEL
In Memory Of
Mr. and Mrs. J. B. Stiles and Rev. and Mrs. S. H. Dimon

FIRST METHODIST CHURCH
Athens, Georgia

John Campbell Stiles · Mary Dimon Stiles
MEMORIAL WINDOW

STILES-DIMON CHAPEL
First United Methodist Church
Athens, Georgia

Career of J. C. Stiles As Hotel Operator Began With Job At $12 Month

JOHN C. STILES, of Athens, Ga., one of the four brot ers comprising the Stiles Hotel Organization, which h leased the Hotel Scott and will operate it in connectic with their other hotel properties. He is experienced every phase of hotel operations and is well known throug out the Southeast.

From $12. a month in 1914—salary on his first hotel job—J. C. Stiles has worked his way up through the hotel business to his present position as head of the Stiles Brothers Corporation, and his newest venture, the opening of the Scott Hotel under the Stiles banner.

The Stiles interests were organized just a few years after 1914 when J. S. Stiles and his brothers and a brother - in - law, W. C. Green, joined forces.

The corporation got into business shortly thereafter and has been very active and successful in the years that have followed. Most of the hotels operated by the corporation are the property Stiles Brothers — the Cherokee in Tallahassee, the Dixie Sherman in Panama City, the Chipola in Marianna, the Redmot in Brimingham, the Air Forest in Union, S. C. the Georgian in Athens and the Baldwin in Milledgeville.

Two additional hotels are operated by the Stiles firm under a lease contract — the Lambuth Inn at Lake Jualuska, North Carolina and the Hotel Scott, which is opening tomorrow.

Since the organization of the corporation the four original owners have seen their sons and nephews grow into manhood and become active members of the firm, interested in the work of managing hotels for their fathers and uncles.

* * *

MR. STILES, in addition to his hotel operations, is very much interested in civic, educational and religious work in his home town of Athens and in the state as a whole is an active Lion in Athens and served Lionism throughout the state, holding several offices in work. He is at the present time a state director in the Georgia Light House for the blind.

His interest in education has taken him to the chairmanship of the Board of Trustees of Reinhardt College. He is also sitting on the Board of Trustees of Young Harris College as the secretary to the board. In addition he is a trustee of the Decatur, Georgia Orphans' Home.

He is a state director in the Georgia Division of the American Cancer Society and in the religious field is very active with the Athens First Methodist Church, which he serves as finance chairman of the Board of Stewards and as chairman of the Sunday School building committee that is sponsoring the erection of a $225,000 Sunday School building of fire proof construction.

Mr. Stiles is chairman of the Board of Conference Claiments of the North Georgia Methodist Conference and was treasurer of the Entertainment Committee at the recent North Georgia conference in Atlanta. He is chairman and treasurer of the Hartwell Youth Center Camp ground of the Athens-Elberton District of the Conference.

* * *

IN ADDITION to his hotel interests, the Georgian is a stock holder and a member of the Board of directors of the Walter R. Thomas Jewelry Company. He owns stock in the Hubert State Banking Company of Athens and serves on its board of directors. He is also affiliated with the Atlanta Wholesale Jewelry Company

ATHENS COUPLE BUILD CHAPEL IN INDIA CONFERENCE

Mr. and Mrs. J. M. Stiles, members of the First Methodist Church of Athens, made a contribution for the erection of a chapel in the South India Annual Conference. The building has been erected and dedicated. It will have a plaque bearing the following inscription: "In Loving Memory of Our Parents, Rev. and Mrs. Stephen H. Dimon, North Georgia Conference From 1878 to 1925. Mr. and Mrs. J. B. Stiles, Milledgeville, Ga. 'Verily There Is A Reward For The Righteous." The following letter has been received by Mr. Stiles from Dr. J. T. Seamands, District Missionary and Conference Evangelist in India.

Jan. 8, 1956

Dear Brother Stiles:

On January 2, we had the thrilling opportunity of dedicating the new vilvage chapel at Hirekodi, built by the money you gave for the purpose. It was a very happy day for that little community. Many non - Christian friends, and the leaders of the vilage, were present on the occasion. The Christians took me in procession into the town and covered me with garlands. I told them I was receiving the garlands in the name of Mr. John Stiles, the donor of the gift. They were pleased at this representation.

I am sending you some pictures taken on the day of dedication. I regret sincerely that the most important picture, the one showing the church from the front, didn't turn out. It's quite a trip to get to the village, so I justcan't run out there at this time and take another picture. But some time in the future when I am out that way, I will try to take another front view picture. The chapel is built of stone, has a cute little verandah, and red tiles. You can see it quite a distance from the village road. I'm sure you would be proud of it.

A few months ago I wrote asking what you wanted to be placed on the plaque, but received no answer to that letter. If you will let me know, we will still do that job for you. We are holding it up, until we get the working from you.

May God bless you richly in 1956 and make you a great blessing. If you want us to take up any further project for you, let us know; we are at your service.

Your Friend, and His,
J. T. Seamands.

TRI-COUNTY ADVERTISER, JULY 8, 1976 PAGE 8

HABERSHAM MILLS IS OLDEST INDUSTRY IN HABERSHAM COUNTY

Marion W. Stribling is President of Habersham Mills.

Aubrey Motz III is Plant Manager of Habersham Mills.

The main office building is another modern addition to Habersham Mills.

This is the way the plant used to look back in the 1890's. Note the rushing water in foreground.

This is an aerial shot of Habersham Mills, which was made in 1966. The plant is located on the site of the old iron works.

Habersham Mills, located at Habersham Georiga, is the oldest industry in Habersham County. The mills occupy a site on which the old Habersham Iron Works and Manufacturing Company once stood. The iron works was incorporated in late 1837, when this section of Georgia was still occupied by the Cherokee. Jarvis Van Buren, a cousin of President Martin Van Buren and a pioneer eastern railroad man, came to Habersham in 1838 to operate the plant for its stockholders, one of whom was John C. Calhoun. The iron mill operated during the War Between the States when guns and cannon were urgently needed for the Confederacy.

The Iron Works closed down in 1882, and Porter Mills, a manufacturer of wool and cotton jean cloth, was located at the site until February 7, 1906. At that time, Habersham Mills purchased the site and approximately 1,200 acres of surrounding property from Porter Mills.

When the mill was purchased mechanical water power was used for its operation. But in 1915, an electrical power system began to be installed. In 1925, a new power plant was built, which produces an approximate 60% of the electrical power required to operate the mill and the surrounding village of some 80 homes which is owned by the mill.

S.Y. Stribling, Sr., was the founder of the mill. His grandson, Marion W. Stribling, is now President of Habersham Mills. Vice President, Assistant Secretary and Treasurer is Reeves Hill. C.L. Pitts is Secretary, and J. T. Gresham is Treasurer. Aubrey Motz III, is Plant Superintendent.

Habersham, Georgia, is an unincorporated town which consists of Habersham Mills property. The mill has its own filter plant and disposal system, as well as its own hydro-electric plants.

Habersham Mills employs 240 workers, and two of them will receive their 50-year pins at the annual Habersham Mills banquet on July 11th. Many of the workers are third-generation employees.

The mills manufacture cotton yarns, and serve an area including Georgia, Alabama, South Carolina, North Carolina, and New England. It consumes 12,000 bales of cotton per year in its yarn production. The yarns are woven into lace goods, towles, narrow fabrics, tapes, backing for plush or pile fabrics, and some ot them are even braided into shoe laces and elastic goods.

Habersham Mills is owned by its stockholders, and continues to be a progressive, thriving industry.

Tri-County Advertiser, Clarkesville, Ga., October 25, 1984

Stribling Honored

Mrs. Kathryn S. Stribling was honored for her outstanding contribution to the Habersham Christian Learning Center at their recent Board of Directors meeting. Mrs. Stribling was given a plaque in commemoration of her instrumental involvement with the center. The plaque states that Mrs. Stribling's efforts "made dreams become realities" with the center.

Mrs. Stribling has been involved from the early days of planning for the learning center. She did a great deal to educate the community about the center concept. Since that time she has been the chairperson of the finance committee, worked with establishing foundation and grant monies, and visited many individuals in the community to raise financial support for the center's work. She as an individual has provided for paving of the parking lot, furnishings for the library and supplied many books. She has also donated many artifacts and art objects for the enjoyment and enrichment of the students. These many achievements are only a few of her rich investments in the center.

Mrs. Sylvia Palmer, director of the learning center stated: "It is by efforts like Mrs. Striblings' that the center has come to be such an integral part of this community. We cannot do enough to celebrate these persons' contributions".

Habersham Christian Learning Center Director Mrs. Sylvia Palmer (right) with Mrs. Kathryn Stribling.

Georgia Mountains, Gainesville, Georgia, Wednesday, October 24, 1984

Honored for work

The board of directors of the Habersham Christian Learning Center has recognized Mrs. Kathryn Stribling for her work with the center. Mrs. Stribling is chairman of the finance committee and has worked to establishing foundation and Nrant money for the center. She has contributed many furnishings and books for the center library. "It is by efforts like Mrs. Stribling's that the center has come to be such an integral part of this community. We cannot do enough to celebrate these person's contributions," said Mrs. Sylvia Palmer, director of the center,

Cornelia Bank

It's great to see some good news about our friends. Congratulations on your recognition....keep up the good work....we're very proud of you!

Bill Loyd

them, 'hollers.' In those days, almost every hollow had a small
stream running through it, and there were many springs either
bubbling up from the ground or coming out of a hillside. There
was one particular spring near where I lived as a boy that had a
large iron pipe driven into the hillside, and the water gushed out
of that pipe in large volume. The stream it created flowed into the
nearby Soque River. The water was cold and pure, slaking the thirst
of many people who traveled on the nearby walking path. Today,
I think that all of the springs and most of the streams are dry."
(Holcomb, p.113)

The book goes on to paint a picture of the set-up of the village,
with the aid of another local with a clear memory. "Situated in
heavily forested land on both sides of the Soque River about three
miles from Clarkesville and two to three miles from Demorest,
the village was a self-contained unit. Birdie Moss remembers:
'Not many families had cars, so the village provided most of the
necessities of life – the mill for employment, houses to live in,
generating plants to produce electricity, a running water system, a
general merchandise store, a post office, an ice plant, a barber shop,
a church and a cemetery.'" (Holcomb, p.113)

We learn by doing in this life. The wise woman next door was
also a big help in my adjustment to this new situation. If I had a
question, I'd ask Kite. Although she was my mother-in-law, the

two of us got along well. Having a helper guide me through the initiation period of transition to a mill life was a must.

I hadn't grown up with animals. Now we had a pack of hunting dogs kenneled in "The Pasture." I'd never been around hunting. Now Marion and his father went bird, rabbit and deer hunting on a regular basis. I'd ridden horses a few times, but not often. Now we had horses right there in the pasture, remarkably close to my bedroom, practically roommates. I'd really only seen chickens on plates after they'd been killed and served as dinner. Now I had a chicken house, right there in the pasture. Who knew that chickens had their own houses? Marion had to come home every day at five to feed the chickens. I was doing well just to feed my husband at that point!

The animals were a large part of the adjustment period, but they were just the first things I noticed. The entire pace of life was slower. I was used to eating in hotel dining rooms. Now Marion came home every day for lunch. And it's not as if there were any restaurants in the mill village. In other words, I had to learn what to do with the water after I'd boiled it. Apparently, that's when you put the food into the pot.

They say that it takes a village to raise a child. At the time, in the world I'd just moved into for life, I was that child. Luckily for me, there happened to be a village. It was full of villagers, all with helpful skills.

My introduction into the pre-set Habersham County class system happened soon after I moved to the county. I thought it would be wonderful to have some of Marion's office employees and their wives over for a nice dinner. "Marion, why don't we invite the supervisors and their wives over for a nice dinner?" I don't know if he knew inside at that moment that this was a bad idea, but he agreed to try, maybe just to placate his new wife. Who knows? Either way, he was right to be hesitant to the suggestions of this wide-eyed, well-meaning, but naïve new-comer.

We did all the things you do when you have one of those business dinners in rural Habersham County. We barbecued chickens. We set a table. We prepared the backyard barbecue pit for a large get-together. We were ready, and then...

It was a complete disaster. No one knew what to say or who to say it to. People fidgeted, attempted small talk, and ate little, all the while counting down the minutes until they could politely make their get-away. I tried to talk about current events, art, literature, but these weren't really parts of their lives. I don't know who was more uncomfortable, them or me. It was probably a tie. They'd never done anything like this, as their social graces were all based on a Baptist Church social life. And here comes this city-girl, this hotel girl wrecking ball, crashing into their world, with her lofty ideas, messing up their carefully-designed apple cart.

Their class system, their world, the miniature designations that dictate the individual steps in their lives had been set down in Habersham long before I arrived on the scene. It was a mill village, built on the rolling hills at the base of the Appalachian Mountains. Each worker and his family paid 50 cents per room per month to live in their houses. The mill houses had two bedrooms, a living room, and a kitchen. The electricity and water costs were taken care of. When I arrived, there were no indoor bathrooms in the village except for the managers' houses, but one of the biggest improvements made by the Striblings' management of the mill village was the installation of indoor plumbing and a septic system. Indoor toilets and baths changed people's lives immeasurably. And so out went the privies and in came 20th century convenience.

There were some amenities and little niceties which made Habersham special. It wasn't the Ritz Carlton, but people had what people needed to live and there was a spirit of community. The Striblings had the only telephone in the area, #1 (our phone number was #1—seriously). People had to come to the house in order to call the doctor or deal with any emergency which required the telephone. The two-story commissary/post-office and group shower/barbershop buildings were popular gathering spots. The men would shower on Saturdays (it was a smellier time) or would gather in the barbershop to talk and relax. I'm not quite sure where the women showered, but I am positive that wherever it was, it was done with a sense of community. The single teacher employed by our elementary school lived in "The Teacherage" on the hill. Although I had rudely discovered that the management and the workers didn't routinely socialize together, otherwise this was a fully-functioning town before I had moved in. Habersham was Mayberry and my husband was the sheriff.

As I've said, buying jewelry at auction was my father's hobby. I wound up inheriting some beautiful diamond pieces from him. Since they were valuable, I thought it wise not to keep them at the house, instead storing them in the mill safe. Other local women kept some jewels there, too. A thief broke into the mill safe once, thinking to snatch the payroll money. Upon finding no payroll there, he wanted something to show for his "labors" and wound up taking my jewelry.

Aspects of the class division seem so blatant now, since I am currently afforded the clearer perspective of looking back at it from a distance of both time and space. For example, the Striblings literally lived at the top of a hill, while the workers lived below. Of course, this being the rural South before the Civil Rights era, there was yet another class division. We had "colored" help, all of whom lived in the neighboring Bean Creek township. The mill was all-white. The nearby small community of Bean Creek was all-black. That was the way it was back then. The men would drive to Bean

Creek on Monday to pick up our two maids, and then drop them back off at home at the end of the week. There was a maid's house in the back of our and Mr. and Mrs. S.Y. Stribling's house, where they would live from Monday through Friday. These maids were paid for their services.

This paternalistic system seems highly patriarchal in retrospect, and it was, but it also worked. When one of our maids became pregnant, she came to us to call the doctor. When she said, "The baby's a'comin', Miss Striblin," I answered, "I'll call the doctor and see if I can get him to come out. In the meantime, I'll come and sit with you." As it turned out, the doctor didn't arrive in time and I wound up delivering the baby myself. This is before I started having babies of my own, so I had no idea of what to do, but we managed somehow. Now that's an initiation into a new place.

My Family

For a ten-year period, every time people saw me I was pregnant. I had five children. For a non-Catholic 20th century Southern family, that was a lot of children. All five pregnancies were easy and went off without any complications.

─────⁂─────

With John Winters, I had gone to Athens for "the event," as we had no hospital in Habersham County at that time. I was staying with my Mother and Daddy at 225 Hampton Court. I had a lot of time on my hands. Marion would come down on the weekends. He would insist that I walk around the block for exercise every evening. It was on one of these visits/walks that I became very uncomfortable, in fact almost unable to make my way back to the house. Later on in the evening we went to St. Mary's hospital, where John was born in the early morning hours. I was completely knocked out during the hard part of labor and knew nothing of the birth. Marion claims that I hollered something awful and that HE suffered a lot. In fact, his first words to me after the ordeal were, "We'll never have another baby! I can't go through this again." We wound up having four more children. Marion survived.

Everyone was jubilant over a boy. Marion had bragged for so long that he was going to have a son that I suppose we would have had to send John back had he been female.

For Jack Stiles' entrance into the world, Marion and I had gone next door to S.Y. and Kite's house to visit and eat liver pudding. She made delicious liver pudding in the cold weather. While there, I was so uncomfortable that I had to lie down on the couch instead of sitting at the table. Later that evening they sent for Dr. D. H. Garrison to come next door to see Mrs. Humphries. We made the call from our house and asked the doctor if he would make one more stop, to check on me. I had reason to believe that my labor might be starting. After checking on me, he advised us to get on the road to Athens immediately, which we did, at a very fast pace. I was timing my contractions in the back seat and Marion was concentrating on arriving before the stork. He drove around the block three times looking for the emergency entrance to St. Mary's. Jack was born in short order with no difficulty. He was a large and strapping baby. I did have back issues after his birth and Jack had a nurse, Miss Moon, to help care for him.

Sloan Yowell III, was a couple of weeks overdue and Dr. Tom Dover decided to induce labor. This took longer, but the birth came naturally with no complications. Sloan was smaller and they kept him in an incubator for a few days.

Dr. Lee Walter delivered Zachary Suddath Stribling. I was at

Mrs. Albert Cobb's at a morning coffee when my water broke. Katherine Bryson, Marion's sister, was visiting and she drove me directly to the new Habersham County hospital. Again, I experienced a very easy birth.

———

Mary Dimon came in the night, and the main thing I remember of that night was how cold I was. I kept asking the nurses for more cover and they finally gave me a hot water bottle. There were great jubilations because, after four boys, we finally had a girl! She was born on the very day of our 11th wedding anniversary.

———

I must have been constructed by nature to be the bearer of many children. I always felt extra good when I was pregnant. In fact, I only recall being sick twice: once when frying fish for supper and once when taking a mortally-wounded dog to the vet.

All five children were breast-fed and cared for by both parents, with no pacifiers. Marion was a hands-on father. He would also bring me coffee in bed during the years when we had all those babies. Getting up was a real chore, after being up and down all the time with those little ones. He would also pitch in with bathing, bottling, feeding and diapering. There was never a better father and husband. I married the most caring man in the world.

———

Early during our first year, I absolutely refused to do any

laundry. My Mother had told me not to ever do the washing, as it was just too hard for any lady. Of course, Mother had never used a washing machine. I soon learned to use one, and, after the second baby we also got a dryer, so I truthfully never sent out the wash.

I didn't learn to drive until after Sloan was born, and I am so glad I did. Neither Mother nor Kite ever learned to drive and were always dependent on someone else to get them around.

Once I began driving the children to and from school in Clarkesville, we had one principal rule in the car. If someone got too rowdy or got into a fight with a sibling, I simply pulled over and stopped the car. That child had to walk the rest of the way home. We did not have many fights in the car. That could be a three-mile walk.

⸺⸱⸱⸺

As my family grew, I had need not for a baby-sitter, but for a baby-chaser. They were all close to each other in age, and, children being children, sitting still wasn't their strong suit. I employed the daughter of a mill employee, a teenaged girl named Sandra Elrod, to chase the babies. She was wonderful, and I'm not sure my sanity would have lasted intact had it not been for Sandra. Her mother even made Mary's clothes. Later, my father paid for Sandra's college tuition for two years at Reinhart College. Sandra went on to get her nursing degree at Emory University.

The Stiles (and Green) Family Barbecue: Pigs Are Wonderful Pets, Especially After You Get Them on the Spit

Everyone was invited. Everyone came. Everyone ate their fill, laughed, and caught up with the people they hadn't seen since the last barbecue.

Once a year, in the fall, when the heat had abated somewhat and the trees were just beginning to turn, the Stiles family hosted a barbecue for everyone we knew. Carl Vinson, the now-legendary Georgia politician and scholar, always came. So did dozens of other hungry people. When the summer ended, they knew to head over to The Green Farm for the annual barbecue/get-together.

They roasted whole pigs. They did it much as their ancestors would have, slow-roasting a pig on a spit, getting up in the middle of the night before the event to get the fire started, butter-flying him, and turning him over and over, preparing to feed a horde of hungry people and their even-hungrier children. The vast expanse of the Green Farm land was littered with children of all ages and descriptions.

The vanishing spirit of The Old South was in full effect on those days. The old men huddled together to tell tall tales. The children played. And the ladies were all proud of the cakes they had prepared. They insisted that Daddy taste each and every cake, a position he readily accepted. His favorite was usually a pound cake.

We've kept the pig-roasting tradition alive in our family. Most American families cook turkeys on Thanksgiving. We cook pig.

We're a barbecue people. We even tried to roast a goat once, but that was mainly out of revenge. Marion decided that he wanted to have a goat...as a pet. As you can imagine, the goat wasn't much of a pet, but I tolerated him...until he ate my hostas. I'd spent countless hours creating a beautiful little garden with multiple plant species (even an import from Ireland), and that goat demolished all my hard work in minutes. Incensed, I laid down the law. "Marion, either that goat goes or I go." Guess who won that battle?

I had the last laugh when I was able to glory in seeing him roasting on our backyard barbecue spit. My revenge wasn't entirely complete however, due to a sudden downpour that forced all of us humans inside, leaving the roasting goat still on the spit. Our dogs demolished ½ of the goat. Chasing them away, the last we saw those dogs were jumping the fence, dragging half a roasted goat behind them.

The half we did eat, though, was delicious.

RELIGION

I WAS REQUIRED TO TAKE AN OLD TESTAMENT COURSE AT Wesleyan and a New Testament course, as well. Even though I had been raised in the church, it was those classes which truly introduced me to the Scriptures. Learning about the history and the details surrounding the passages I'd heard many times as a child filled in many of the gaps in my early religious education.

My father was an ardent supporter of the Methodist Church. He gave generously of his time, talents and money to the church. Wherever we moved, we were still Methodists. Families who move around a lot tend to cling to the constants in their lives. For the Stiles, the one looming constant was the Methodist Church. Being Georgians, the historical tie with the Wesley brothers and the other founders of the colony gave us a sense of pride and history.

Later in life Daddy clung even tighter to his religion and built the Stiles-Dimon Chapel at Athens First Methodist Church and, at the same time, built a mission church in India (So, if you're ever in India, drop by, sing a hymn, and take a picture of the place.). Daddy was also the Chairman of the Board of Trustees for Young Harris College and LaGrange College, both Methodist institutes of higher learning. At one time he was even the Chairman of the Board of the "Conference Claimants" of the North Georgia Methodist Church. If you're Methodist, that means a lot to you. If you're not, you probably have no idea what that is, but trust me, it's a big deal.

As for my personal religious history, when I moved to Habersham, I joined the Methodist Church in Clarkesville, the closest church of my denomination. I was a regular, singing in the choir, playing the brass bells, and once, I even took on the unenviable task of presiding over the Women's Work in the church. Along with everything else, I ran the church blood drives, coordinating between the church elders, the parishioners and the American Red Cross, and finding other volunteer "workers" to handle the rather large amount of secretarial work that comes with a blood drive.

In small town churches, you usually sit in the same pew every week. As Marion and I had children and the Stribling family began to expand, we eventually took up a full row, the second pew, center aisle, almost overflowing from our station with two adults and five children, as well as Kite.

I think it's important for children to take an active role in the life of the church. During those Toccoa summers I attended many Vacation Bible Schools, summer religious programs which catered to all Protestant denominations: Presbyterian, Methodist, Baptist, and others. We'd learn the same Bible stories, sing the same hymns and drink the same grape juice. The lessons I learned there have stayed with me, and I've tried to impart them to my own children.

I never heard my father utter a "curse word." Nor would he and my mother countenance anyone around them using foul language. They were also tee-totalers, even refusing to serve alcohol in their hotels. The ideals of Methodist Christianity permeated many aspects of my childhood. Consequently, I never touched alcohol myself until after I was married. The Striblings were social drinkers, by no means abusers of alcohol, but they had a few cocktails when the occasion called for it.

My Second Dose of Academia

THE SECOND TIME I VENTURED INSIDE THE HALLOWED IVORY towers of American academia it took. The first time I was too caught up in life, too excited to be on my own for the first time, and too interested in boys to concentrate on my studies. However, on June 2nd, 1968 I graduated from Piedmont College in Demorest, Georgia, at age 42.

In my forties, after having birthed and raised five children, I decided to change directions in life, to go back to school and to get my degree. I may have been swimming upstream culturally as a middle-age student, but I bested the current. In truth, I thoroughly enjoyed being a student the second time and wound up graduating with a double major in English Literature and European History, even making the Dean's List. It helped my grades immensely that I was less preoccupied with looking at boys this time.

By some curious circumstance, some strange turn of events, I wound up graduating alongside my oldest son, John. Since, by some more understandable circumstance, John and I have the same last name, we were right next to each other in our graduate class photograph.

Not many mothers can claim that they were in the same grade as their oldest child, and though it was largely no big deal, my academic success did cause one or two minor headaches. One day on campus, John overheard a young man talking about Professor Blah-Blah-Blah's habit of grading on a curve. He went on to complain that, "If we didn't have that old bitch in the class, we'd be okay." As a dutiful Southern son, John couldn't let this stand. He approached the young man, intercepted him, and told him, in no uncertain terms, "That old bitch is my mother." That shut him up!

I Needed Something to do with My Hands

"People who think needlepoint is just one stitch after another don't know needlepoint."

In the late 1970's, I picked up a new hobby, needlepoint. For the next 20 years, until my sight failed me, I learned, experimented and perfected the art of needlepoint. Southern ladies have often learned how to embroider and do needlepoint as a way to create lovely and useful designs to decorate homes, offices and even mill buildings. In the 70's, I joined their ranks...out of boredom.

I didn't like the beach. I've never been able to sunbathe due to my blonde complexion. I've neither had the athleticism nor the desire to surf or build sand castles. But that does not mean we didn't venture to the ocean, many times in the history of our family vacations. The children and Marion enjoyed playing in the surf, leaving me with some time on my hands. Needing something to do while my family was frolicking in the salty surf, I taught myself to stitch. My first purchase and project was an eye glass case, purchased while at the beach.

As with any new hobby, especially ones that become as addictive as needlepoint, it started small and grew exponentially. Next, I made a bell pull, using a design imported from London, England. At the time, the U.S. didn't sell the packets needed to stitch intricate patterns. I kept on learning, making more and more intricate patterns. Eventually, I got to the point where I was routinely stitching wall hangings. It became "my thing." I could stitch words I wanted on pretty much anything. Like any other artist, I always signed and dated my work. The only piece of advice I would give is to sign and date your work.

TRAVEL

EARLY IN OUR MARRIAGE MARION WAS INVITED BY A TEXTILE machinery cartel to visit Stuttgart, Germany. He and other textile men from around the globe were asked to experience a revolutionary new cotton yarn spinning frame. The German company wanted to introduce the new system to America, and the way to do that was to first get textile executives excited, letting them see it in action. Marion told the cartel, "I'd love to go, but I don't travel without my wife." You've gotta love a man like that!

This was an extremely fancy experience. We were chauffeured around Stuttgart in a limousine, the driver dropping Marion off at the textile plant and taking me to visit interesting cathedrals and other local sites. There was, however, a distinct language barrier. I didn't speak German, and he didn't speak English. Consequently, I didn't learn as much as I would have otherwise, but those were some beautiful cathedrals. Other than not providing us a driver who could communicate with us in a way that didn't involve excessive gesticulation and drawing stick figures, those folks catered to our every whim. Upon learning that I'd never been to London, they insisted on making us a reservation for the trip home. We flew into Heathrow Airport and I was bathed once again in the familiar sounds of our native tongue, before spending an extravagant weekend at the Dorcester Hotel, perhaps the most luxurious 5-Star hotel I'd ever seen.

I didn't know it at the time, but I had just been bitten by the travel bug. I've ridden camels in Egypt and The Canary Islands. I've ridden an elephant in India. I've air-ballooned over France. I've ridden the rails through most of Europe and parts of Asia. I've taken a boat up the Nile. I rode a donkey in Greece. I've eaten kangaroo in Australia. And I've walked on the Great Wall of China. Suffice it to say, I've been around.

Although I certainly attended school as a child and a young adult, it was my adult travels that truly made me interested in learning. I was also raised in the church, but it wasn't until I started traveling later in life and searching out the holy sites of other religions, studying the rituals and beliefs of world religions, that I gained a true appreciation for my own Methodism. Mark Twain called travel the "antidote for prejudice," and, as an avid traveler whose pseudonym was based on a riverboat industry term, he ought to have known. That certainly was true for me. I don't think I was prejudiced, especially having met so many different types of people in the hotels of my youth, but travel was an eye-opening experience for me.

I wouldn't have made a very good missionary. I never wanted to convert the people I met to my religion. Quite the opposite, in fact. I always wanted to learn all I could about their religions, reading up on them before the trips and visiting holy shrines and places of worship on the trips. I've gone through the motions of Hinduism and Islam. I even have a Muslim prayer rug. I may be the only person to have ever both lived in Habersham County and owned a Muslim prayer rug.

———

The key to successful travel is research. Always learn about the place you're going to visit before you go, otherwise you'll miss out on half the experience. Learn about the culture. Learn at least a little of the language. Learn the currency exchange rates. And don't forget to learn the country's customs. For example, I traveled to the Soviet Union once and discovered that it is not proper in Russia to tip your waiter in cash. However, leaving little non-monetary tips on the table is common practice. I tipped many waiters with many tubes of lipstick.

Even if you cannot learn to speak the native tongue, you can at least learn how to say a few helpful phrases. "Where's the bathroom?" comes to mind. Learning how to ask for directions will almost surely be useful. Even if the person you ask has to answer you in pantomime, you're going to need to know how to get around. You're also probably going to want to eat and sleep on your trip, so learn some hotel- and food-related linguistic tidbits.

———

Personally, I benefited from the abundant research material furnished by the Smithsonian Institute for the trips sponsored by that revered American historical institution, but there are many other means of research. The Smithsonian sent us lists of books, which we would then check out of our local libraries. Having fun and knowledgeable tour guides like John and Nancy Kollock helped, too.

Travel Even in the Face of
Potential Nuclear Fallout

The explosion at the Chernobyl nuclear power plant in the 1980s in what was then the U.S.S.R. was headline news everywhere in the world, except of course IN the Soviet Union. I was a part of a travel group on our way to Warsaw at the time, traveling with a group of newspaper editors and journalism graduate students. Being a regular newspaper contributor got me included in this group. Being friends with the organizer helped, too. He was a Russian professor at Emory University in Atlanta. When they told me about the trip, however, I don't recall their saying anything about a nuclear explosion. Honestly, I would've gone anyway.

We heard about Chernobyl when our plane had just landed in Germany, and so we had the option of turning around and heading home or staying the course. The future was uncertain. The atmosphere was tense and cloudy in more ways than one. The toxic cloud of death was blowing toward Scandinavia. We all phoned our families. They all told us to come home. Lord knows, that's what Marion told me. I didn't want to go back. No one else in the group did either. We were intrepid travelers. It would take more than a nuclear explosion for me to change my travel plans.

Looking back now with the clear eyes of nostalgic remembrance, I can say that I've been everywhere I wanted to go. I have traveled the globe, seen amazing sights, embraced new and exotic cultures, tasted exotic foods, learned about foreign religions, tried my hand at new customs, and broadened myself using the best method yet known to man--travel.

DOMESTIC TRAVEL

AMERICA IS HUGE. THERE'S SO MUCH IN THIS VAST LAND OF OURS that it's impossible to fit it all in one lifetime. That doesn't mean that I haven't tried.

Being in the textile industry afforded me the chance to attend annual conferences of trade associations, The Georgia Textile Manufacturers and The American Yarn Spinners. The top executives from around the country would meet annually, compare notes, swap secrets, attend lectures and expositions, and get to know each other in interesting surroundings. These conferences were always held in resort tourist locations. Having been raised as a hotel child, this was my territory. I felt completely at home in hotels in Boca Raton, Florida or Sea Island, Georgia.

We went to Hawaii one year. It's hard for most people not to be impressed by Hawaii, but by now you should realize that I am not most people. Other than the Pearl Harbor memorial, which is awe-inspiring, I found Hawaii to be a more expensive version of South Florida. I got a lot of needlepoint done on that trip.

We gathered for these conferences all over the country. One year it was The Fairmont Hotel in San Francisco. Another year it was the Arizona desert. During the year when Marion was the president of the G.T.M.A. (Georgia Textile Manufacturers Association), he took the convention to the thin air and snow-drenched ski paradise of the Rocky Mountains, specifically The Broadmoor Hotel in Colorado Springs, Colorado. The entire family went on this trip and we had a wonderful time.

FAMILY TRAVEL

IT WASN'T ALL TRADE SHOWS. MARION AND I TOOK THE children on various family vacations, too. Normally, Marion took a week off from work, I took time off whichever committees I was on at the time, and we traveled to different locations, usually resorts in Florida.

We had family gatherings in Panama City early on at the Dixie Sherman hotel run by Walter Green (Daddy's brother-in-law) and his sons. Daddy had a lease at the Sir Charles Motel in Jacksonville Beach and we went there as well. For a brief time Daddy even owned a cottage in Panama City, Florida. Clifford Stiles bought a house on the beach at the same time and in future years his family afforded us the chance to make many family vacation memories at that beach house. The Clifford Stiles grandchildren run the house now.

I was comfortable in hotels, so it was never as big an adjustment for me as it was for my children. If our accommodations happened to be in a cottage, I'd bring in groceries and cook in the kitchen. For every day we spent in a family cottage on the beach I'd diligently purchase a gallon of milk, a pound of bacon, and a loaf of bread. Cooking breakfast and lunch on vacation saves money and saves time. Access to a swimming pool was always a plus, too.

When Alwyn and I sold the Georgian Hotel property, I received a good-sized amount of money. Knowing that this would be the largest chunk of money I'd ever see at one time, I spent part of it on future memories, taking the whole family (children, husband, in-laws, grandchildren, everybody) on a Caribbean cruise on the *SS Norway*.

We didn't always go to the beach. We sometimes mixed it up and traveled to Lake Junaluska, that mountain resort and Methodist Mecca where I'd spent so much time in my youth.

My brother Alwyn bought a small cabin on Lake Burton. When my children were younger, we enjoyed visiting, and the children loved playing in the lake. Years later, the family, under the direction of Alwyn's children made that small cabin into a two-story gorgeous lake mansion. Alwyn let my family use the lake house one week a year in the summer. Again, many memories were made there.

CHARITY:

GIVING BACK

AS MY FATHER HAD TAUGHT ME, THROUGHOUT MY LIFE I HAVE tried to adhere to the Christian notion of, "To whom much is given, much is expected." Since I have been given much, I have felt the need to give back an equal measure. Not to in any way boast, because humility is a Christian virtue as well, I only mention my charity work to inspire others to do the same. There is always someone in need of charity, and not only have I always taken that lesson to heart, I believe that I have successfully passed the idea on to my children.

My own spirit of giving has taken many forms over the years: volunteering for numerous church committees, bringing the idea of helping the less fortunate to Habersham County, setting up rural Christian education, organizing a school for the mentally-challenged residents of Habersham County, and being a part of so many other random school and religious committees that I can barely remember them all. One skill I have always possessed is the ability to raise money. No matter what type of charity it is, no matter the cause, the size or the scope of the endeavor, they all inevitably have one thing in common. They all need money. I cut my teeth selling advertising space for my high school yearbook, and I discovered back then I was pretty good at it. It's a skill I have honed with practice, lots and lots of practice. In the process, I've been able to help many needy Georgians.

My two largest-scale charity projects in my attempt to effect positive change in Habersham County involved setting up The Habersham Christian Learning Center and in organizing a school for the mentally-challenged.

I won't go into all of the minute details, but I do want to write a little about these undertakings which are so close to my heart.

In the middle of the 20th century there weren't always schools for mentally-challenged children or adults. Often individuals who had been labeled "retarded" by doctors and/or school officials were pushed to the fringes of society, forced to make do with handouts and lives with very little mental and emotional fulfillment. They were more often seen as burdens or crosses to bear than as human beings with the ability to contribute to their communities. I disagreed. Shortly after arriving in the region, I began to notice the need for a special school for the mentally-disabled population of Habersham County. Never one to sit on my laurels, I began to act.

The Jaycettes were the female equivalent of the Jaycees, an American charitable organization with a long and storied history. I was approached by the Jaycette leader and asked to add my name and abilities to this noble cause. Instead of merely writing a check or volunteering a few hours of time here and there, I jumped in with both feet. President Jimmy Carter was the governor of Georgia at the time. He and his passionate activist wife, former First Lady Rosalind Carter, were proponents of change in the way we treat mentally-challenged children and adults. It was Rosalind Carter's pet project, an undertaking close to her heart. The timing could not have been better.

There was no opportunity for schooling and very few opportunities for enrichment at all for the mentally-handicapped population of the area. They couldn't attend "normal" school. Nobody wanted to ship them to schools in Atlanta or somewhere else that far away. We needed a local school. In order to get one, we needed to raise awareness, and, in order to raise awareness, we first needed to raise money. With the help of the local Jaycette chapter, I planned a barbecue on The Hill to bring attention to this fact. We invited the movers and shakers of the area, the people capable of bringing about the necessary change, to the event. It was well-known in Habersham that if you tempt people with Stribling barbecue, they'll come out of the woods for a taste. They'd knock down their grandmothers to get some of our famous barbecue.

The people responded as expected. The Hill was teeming with influential locals that afternoon. As the final touches were being added to the roasting chickens, we watched the police escort surrounding Georgia's First Lady make its slow way up The Hill. Mrs. Carter was passionate about the project and a gracious guest to our home. She spoke eloquently about the need for schools like these, beautifully summarizing the spirit of charity.

"A civilization is judged on the basis of the attention it gives to its most helpless citizens."

Her words rang true. If everyone were as charitable as Rosalind and Jimmy Carter the world would be a kinder place.

Mrs. Carter's presence certainly helped the cause, but the barbecue was just one footnote in a longer struggle. I was close with the editor of the local newspaper, Amalie Graves, having written numerous articles, mostly focusing on ways we could improve our little corner of the world. She published a few pleas for help I'd written for the need for a school and a care center for mentally-retarded children. I wrote up a speech and put together a slide show to tug on people's heart-strings. I started a local Special Olympics. We hired the requisite Special Education teachers. Needing the proper space, we converted an abandoned education building of the Bethlehem Baptist Church into a "Day Care" center for mentally-challenged children. This mission filled so much of my time. I became so immersed in this challenge that I even earned college credits and was awarded a degree in Special Education.

I am equally proud of the role I played in establishing and maintaining The Habersham Christian Learning Center, Inc. This mission, this quest, was a long time in the making and took the support of many influential locals and religious leaders. Georgia Superior Court Judge Jack Gunter's 1967 speech about the need for regional Christian education is thought to have been the initial inspiration in our area of the country. Judge Gunter spoke of the need for "released-time" Christian centers, built with local church support instead of tax money, with full-time Christian educators, and courses designed to include not only Bible studies, but also to help students learn to incorporate Christian lessons into their everyday lives. Gainesville attorney Sam Harben, Jr. was present for that speech, and he and Sylvia Palmer brought the idea of interweaving Christian principles into America's public school system to our area when she and her husband Gerald moved to Habersham County. The Palmers planted the seed in the minds of the residents, in the hearts of the local churches, and even into the agenda of the local Board of Education. Habersham residents from nine cities and churches of various denominations (Methodists, Baptists, Presbyterians, Episcopalians, and Catholics) all pitched in to make this dream a reality, as did specialty, secular, and civic clubs like the Chamber of Commerce, The Rotary Club, the Cornelia Garden Club, the Kiwanis Club, the Wisteria Club and the local United Way chapter, among others. Even the owner of The Steak

House, Bobby Joe Caudell, offered free meals to anyone who came to one of our consciousness- and fund-raising talks.

The Cornelia United Methodist Church, under the leadership of the man who was Marion's best friend, Calvin Stovall, began promoting the idea first, with my own Clarkesville United Methodist Church next heeding the call, and with the financial and time commitments of these churches' respective preachers, leaders, and the aid of and of course, a lot of work on my own part (which took the form of heavy financial support, plenty of volunteer hours, floral decoration, and even agreeing to serve on the board of directors for four years), we all did eventually turn this dream into a reality...but we almost didn't. We ran into financial snags, such as forgetting to budget for the initial building plan. We discovered design snags, such as discarding our initial ideas for building materials in favor of the more cost-effective and attractive choice of a metallic building. We expected to encounter some problems, but we never expected to hit a legal snag in our very religiously observant rural area. After years of planning, effort, and sweat, including my paying for the Dimon Memorial Library (obviously, I named the library -- a fitting tribute I think) as well as all of the other furnishings in the building, we thought that we were set to go.

On the very day that our dedicated group of Christian educators began to accept construction bids, we ran straight into the legal swamp of "separation of church and state." That same day, a

Clarkesville lawyer threatened to sue us were we to proceed.

Though it probably goes without saying, this was a spiritual crusade, and, since it was also located adjacent to the school grounds, we could not avoid and thus had to deal with the issue of the separation of church and state. We hired a lawyer to avoid "church and state" legal entanglements (sometimes, no exaggeration, having to literally take one step to the left to talk about religious issues and then switch to scholastic language when we took one step to the right). We hired Sylvia Palmer as our first Director and first High School teacher. She was a talented teacher and Christian activist. With plenty of help from others, including myself, Sylvia oversaw this project from start to finish.

The legal dance we engaged in wouldn't have been necessary if we weren't adjacent to public school grounds, but it's a small community with limited resources, and we made the best of what we had. Although when we set out on this quest we naively believed that the whole community would be behind us, we ran into so many problems that I was quoted in the History of Habersham Christian Learning Center, Inc's 2002 publication as saying, "This just seems to go from one crisis to another." I won't list all of the other issues we ran into, but I would like to make a quick plug for the value of determination. Famed anthropologist Margaret Meade once said, "Never doubt that a small and dedicated group of people can change the world."

When the dust settled, the funds were secured, the community was lined up behind the project, and the parents were properly notified, we had 10 students on that January day in 1982, our first year. The school is still in operation today and has, over the years, taught countless moral lessons, given scholarships to many deserving students and been a needed sanctuary for too many teenagers to count. I am understandably proud of all of this.

More Milling around

In 1977 The Russell Corporation acquired Habersham Mills. Marion stayed on to run the mill, overseeing operations as he'd always done, and managing the transition. At the time the mill employed around 250 people, all of whose lives were about to drastically change. When the Russell Corporation finally closed the mill's doors in 1999, the labor force had dwindled to around 150 people. Corporate ownership changes things.

Russell changed the product line from 2-ply cotton yarn to single-ply cotton/rayon/polyester knitting yarn, which was popular at the time. It wasn't long until all of the production migrated West to Russell's main center of operations in Alexander City, Alabama, where they used Habersham yarn to make T-shirts, sweatshirts, sweatpants and other knit apparel.

In 1979 Russell installed new equipment, with my husband overseeing the transition. With Marion's steady hand to guide the new direction, eight years later, in 1988, the company made yet another major overhaul, installing state-of-the-art machinery and renovating to accommodate the new and much heavier equipment. The floors had to be reinforced to prevent the building's sinking into the ground due to the added weight. The new machinery and new direction brought a new process known as "open-ended spinning" to Habersham, thus eliminating the need for a number of jobs and employees. The job loss of this production streamlining was handled by natural attrition and not through directly laying off employees.

Russell brought the practices, identity and mindset of large corporation to the daily operation of the mill. The employees who stayed on with Russell received a higher pay scale, better benefits and an upgraded retirement plan, but, despite these improvements, this was a difficult transition for many of the workers. Their world was changing around them, and they felt an understandable sense of sadness and loss that their old, familiar surroundings, management style and work processes were now very different.

In 1906, and for a time afterward, the mill had employed the majority of the county and had the largest payroll in the area. Even by 1977, when the sale was finalized, the mill was one of the most visible and most influential mainstays in the county. During all of the decades under Stribling management there was a true family feel to the running of the mill, a kinship brought about by a tight-knit group of people in a relatively isolated place, all working toward the same goal, the production of high-quality yarn. The corporate mentality that Russell brought in changed everything. Because of the impact that Habersham Mills had on the area, and in tribute to the Stribling family – whose name became synonymous with the mill – the General Assembly of the State of Georgia, on February

21, 1992, honored the Striblings with the adoption of a resolution designating the bridge across the Soque River on Habersham Mills Road as the "Stribling Memorial Bridge."

When the Russell Corporation closed the mill's doors in 1999, Sloan Stribling II, my son, was still employed by the mill, bringing once and for all an end to a long and successful Stribling legacy of management and employment with the mill. During the entire span of Stribling association -- 93 years -- at least one member of the family, sometimes several, was employed at some position within the framework of the mill.

For years it had been common practice at Habersham Mills that employees who lived in a mill house and had retired were allowed to continue living in their old houses as long they continued to draw breath. This is a shining example of the generosity of a family-run business model. Shortly after the mill closed down, the families who were living in mill houses received notification that they had to move within a designated period of time. Even Marion and I, after 52 years of married life in the same house on "The Hill" had to relocate. We moved to Hollywood, Georgia, into a beautifully-designed home with a 180-degree panoramic view of our beloved North Georgia mountains.

Marion put it best. "I had to move. I simply couldn't bring myself to drive by the mill and not hear that old familiar hum of the machinery."

⁓

Things change. If there's one constant in life it is that there are no constants. Things inevitably change. The ability to be able to bend with the times is a useful trait. Marion was a man who learned how to "roll with the punches." Even so, he didn't want to have to experience a daily reminder of this change every time he exited the village.

THE FINAL FRONTIER:
TRAVELING ON TO GREENER PASTURES

MY PARENTS, CONSTANTLY ON THE MOVE IN LIFE, RELOCATING periodically from city to city, from hotel to hotel, have, at the time of my writing this book, both since passed on to that 5-Star hotel in the sky. Although the medical causes of their deaths were essentially the same, the details of their respective passings and the effects on their remaining loved ones could not have been more different.

While in Thomasville, Georgia, in the midst of the laborious process of preparing yet another hotel, The Scott Hotel, for its grand opening, John Stiles suffered his first stroke. Seventeen long and painful years went by from that moment until his eventual demise. This was a period full of doctors, an era of extended hospital stays, a time of a multitude of caregivers and an epoch of declining physical and mental capabilities. Daddy had always been my rock, a steely and steady presence in my life, someone I turned to when times were rough. Needless to say, it was a difficult time for me.

This long good-bye took its toll on every member of the family. We all suffered along with him. The family business was taken over by my brother, Alwyn. As was the custom with family businesses, the son took the reins when the father could not hold them any longer. My parents' final place of residence, their apartment in that upscale Athens mainstay, The Georgian Hotel, was sold and converted to condominiums. The condominiums remain there to this day, though the owners of the street-level restaurant have recently attempted to refurbish the lobby in the same style I remember from my high school days in the war years.

My mother's passing was far more fortunate for her and far less painful for the rest of the family. Like her husband, my mother, Mary Dimon Stiles, suffered a stroke. Unlike her husband, however, Mother did not have to suffer for very long before passing on. After her stroke, she checked into the hospital. Two short days later, she passed away. Though I and the entire family, naturally, lamented the loss of such a beautiful, talented and generous woman, we were simultaneously grateful that, unlike Daddy, she did not have to linger in pain for very long. My mother based her life on the solid biblical principles she inherited from her parents.

Much like my father, my husband Marion Stribling's passing took a long time. After being diagnosed with Multiple Myeloma (a type of cancer said to be incurable) and being told by the doctors that he had but two years to live, Marion proved them wrong and held on for eight years. He was always strong in life. Marion spent those last seven years being treated chemically and surgically for his cancer. Sloan, living in Habersham county at the time, was my go-to person as Marion's health slowly and steadily declined. Sloan maintained our home when we couldn't and spent many nights comforting me after Marion's eventual passing.

The greatest tragedy anyone can ever suffer in life is not the death of parents or a spouse. The death of any loved one is trying, but there is nothing in this life more tragic than losing a child. Children are supposed to outlive their parents. My son Jack's passing was the hardest thing I ever had to endure. Jack Stiles Stribling was my second oldest child. Like his father, Jack died of cancer. He was diagnosed with esophageal cancer and died 18 days later. He lived long enough to leave behind a grieving wife, two wonderful daughters and Annie, his beloved granddaughter. When Jack passed from this Earth in 2014, all of us grieved.

FAMILY SECRETS

I'M NOT ABOUT TO EXPOSE HIDDEN SECRETS. THIS IS NOT A LIST of long-hidden Stiles and Stribling family clandestine lore. Instead, in looking back over my life as a natural aspect of writing this memoir, I have not been able to help but note that I've been a member of two successful families. Judging from the ever-climbing divorce rate in America and the amount of people in therapy over childhood trauma, I can safely claim that not everyone gets so lucky. However, it wasn't all luck. It takes hard work to create a successful family, and, despite the current trajectory toward gender equality, the majority of the burden for fostering happy and prosperous family atmospheres still falls squarely on the shoulders of the wife and mother.

What did I learn?

What can I tell you?

If I had to list one piece of advice it would be to plan a date night with your spouse. It sounds simple, but it makes a world of difference. Marion and I set aside one night a week to go out to dinner with friends. We continued this tradition for over 30 years. Children are a blessing, but adults need to be in the company of other adults, in a place where no diapers are permitted. Marion and I had a standing Friday night dinner date with four other couples: Judge and Mrs. Jack Adams, Mr. and Mrs. Bill Shortt, Jack and

Edna Ellard, and Calvin and Nancy Stovall. The physical location changed, but the line-up remained stable. We'd meet in a restaurant or at one of our houses. All of the men had served in World War II, and we were all raised in Georgia, so we had a lot in common. Plan a date night. It helps.

There may not be one specific model for wedded bliss. My parents had a long and successful marriage and they got married in the middle of the night. Daddy desperately wanted to marry my mother, but he couldn't spare much time off work. It was World War I and most of his male employees were "over there" battling the Kaiser, so Daddy, as he always did, took it on himself and shouldered most of the work. Not able to leave his post, but eager to marry my lovely mother, the two of them were wed by my grandfather, the Revered Stephen Dimon, in the middle of the night. Their honeymoon was non-existent. They had to beat it back to The Baldwin Hotel for work the very next morning.

RECENTLY:

FULL CIRCLE

I AM RAPIDLY APPROACHING MY 92ND YEAR ON THE PLANET. FOR the past twelve years I have lived at The Iris Place, an independent living facility in Athens, Georgia. I'm quite content with this arrangement. My children visit often. My daughter, Mary, oversees my care. She now works as the Sales Leader here at The Iris Place. My son Zachary is her back up to help me and brings me homemade banana bread almost every week. My son Sloan has held down the fort in Habersham. My son John oversees the family estate and my financial holdings. We see the Jack Stribling family on holidays.

<hr style="width:10%" />

I suppose my life expectations are now centered around my three great grandchildren, Parker, Kite, and Annie. I love hearing of their activities. All are proving to be special in their own ways.

<hr style="width:10%" />

We operate well as a family unit, just as we did when Marion was still alive, just as I did within my own birth family. It seems as if I have essentially come full-circle, from living in hotel apartments in my youth to my one-bedroom apartment in my golden years.

STILES GENEAOLOGY

A SMALL, HAND-SEWN, PAPER-COVERED VOLUME OF STILES genealogy, from the Connecticut branch of the family, containing perhaps our most illustrious ancestor, Ezra Stiles (UGA founder, Yale president, and prominent colonial-era pastor) was published around the year 1762. On its title page appeared this prologue:

A Genealogical Collection of that
FAMILY OF STILES which
Came from Milbroke in Bedfordshire
In Great Britain 1634
And settled at Windsor in the Colony

Of Connecticut in New England, 1636,

At a Time when

In twelve years from 1629 to 1641

Four Thousand Men with about Three Thousand Families

Implying Fifteen or Twenty Thousand Souls

For the sake of free Exercise of Pure Religion

Fled out of England from the Tyranny & Persecution

Of King Charles the first and A B P Land

And settled in New England

Where their Posterity

In the year 1760 the year of the English Conquest

Of Canada, were increased to half a Million Souls.

Our Family of Stiles was one of this

Original Accession & purely

English Blood;

A LEGACY

LUCILLE CANDLER DIMON

1892-1981

By Kathryn Stribling

~:~

In December, 1980, when a little lady died in Habersham

Home, room #114, there were but few belongings to bundle up.

A framed picture of John and Patricia Alden – a memento of

happier days – a wall-mounted TV, which she had enjoyed from her

bed; a radio from her sister, permanently set on a station featuring

classical music – a music box from a great nephew – a record

player – nightgowns, bedjackets and robes, a mute testimony of

many years of illness. And a Bible: grey, worn, pencil-marked in

the margins, heavy underlined, whole sections loose from the spine

from repeated use. A student's Bible, and on the front page, "From

Papa – Christmas, 1920."

No great estate, certainly. No estate taxes to be paid. No will to probate. Then...what was her legacy? What did she leave to you and me? Because we are still here today, you must think it was something of value that you still cherish. Something unique that you recognized in her during her years of teaching in a Sunday School classroom. But I cannot address myself to this, for I never heard Lucille Dimon teach. During my lifetime I never heard her expositate on a single scripture or moralize to an adolescent and a somewhat-willful niece on the virtue of "The Good Book." She was far too wise for that.

But always for me, a city- and hotel-bred child, wherever she was, was "Home." The first I remember was in Toccoa where I was delivered in the front room. One of the thousands of Dr. Ayers' babies. This is where we came for Christmas, for summer vacations, for birthdays, and all the "family times." A retired ("super-annuated" I believe is the term), Methodist preacher's home is certainly not the most prestigious in town. But the memories I have are of great fun, for we had a well-spring of life and activity, of picnics and hot biscuits – which Teal turned out in succulent heaps – of backyard circuses curtained by sheets and "helped along" backstage by her hands – Christmas morning waking up snug and warm in her bed – as we conspired together about the "secret surprises" planned for the day. This was "Home." Security – love lavishly given, unquestioned acceptance...the richest legacy for any child.

Then, during my high school years, Teal and her sister, Claudia, moved to Mt. Airy to a little cottage which my father had bought, both for them and as a summer retreat for my mother, my brother and myself. These were the war years, paratroopers from Camp Toccoa, Navy and Army Signal Corps men from Athens. Many found their way to "Green Peace Cottage." Some came initially as my "dates," but stayed on because they, too, had found a "Home." Long after I had returned to school they were eating dinner with two old maids. They knew a good thing when they found it. Some hitchhiked from Athens to Toccoa. Letters from their grateful mamas back home in New York, Arizona, or wherever were ample evidence that they had discovered what "Southern Hospitality" was all about.

Many of her school students from the Mt. Airy and Toccoa teaching years came by to see her when she was at Habersham Home. Several were nurses who cared for her needs. Without exception, they spoke of her as "the kindest and best teacher they ever had." Far from being permissive, her classroom was a model of order and discipline, kindness, patience, intelligence, fun-loving – I bet you didn't know she taught a class of folk-dancing...all were hallmarks of her character. I can truly say that I have never heard her speak ill of any person.

⁓

No, I was never one of her students in school or church. But I have a far greater legacy. She demonstrated in her home, by the manner in which she lived, and by her courage and faith through her long years of illness, more about the Christian way of life than is expressed by any theology or creed. Truly...she walked in the Master's steps.

Now, several months after her passing, we have seen the beginning of The Habersham Christian Learning Center established in our area. I have initially funded the nucleus of the Library Fund for the Center as a living memorial to her. For it is an idea that I believe she would have richly approved of. For that is what she achieved through her career of teaching both young and old; "THE CHRISTIAN WAY, THE TRUTH, AND THE LIGHT"...That she not only taught, that she truly personified... That is what she was all about.

[[This excellent legacy was presented by Kathryn Stribling, niece of Miss Dimon, at the Sunday School Assembly of the Crusaders Class on Sunday, May 17, 1981. Miss Dimon was co-founder and first teacher of the class and continued teaching for over 15 years. On this day, she was also memorialized by charter members of the class and a portrait of her was hung in the classroom as a token of love and appreciation for the wonderful legacy she left to all of us as well as to the entire membership of Cornelia United Methodist Church.]]

A TRIBUTE
published in the pages of
THE DAILY NEWS
ATHENS, GA.
JUNE 4 1974

Memorial Obituary

Entered Into Eternal Rest
Monday, June 3, 1974

Retired executive

John Stiles dies at 80

John Campbell Stiles, of 125 Beachum Drive, a retired hotel executive and an Athens resident for the past 40 years, died Monday after a lengthy illness. He was 80.

A native of Baldwin County, he was a former president of Stiles Hotel Company, which operated hotels in five southeastern states. He was a member of First United Methodist Church here and was active as a layman in the North Georgia Conference.

He served as chairman of the board of trustees of Reinhardt College and was a member of the boards of trustees for Young Harris College, LaGrange College and the Methodist Children's Home in Decatur. He was also chairman of the board of Conference Claimants.

Funeral services will be held Wednesday at 11 a.m. at First United Methodist Church, with the Revs. Dr. Cecil Myers and Arthur O'Neal Jr. officiating. Burial will be in Memory Hill Cemetery in Milledgeville Wednesday at 3:30 p.m.

Pallbearers will include Alwyn Barry Stiles Jr., Jack Stiles Stribling, J.C. Green, John Stribling, Sloan Stribling III and Zachary Stribling, with the Forum Class of the First United Methodist Church serving as honorary pallbearers.

Survivors include his widow, the former Mary Haygood Dimon; a daughter, Mrs. Marion Stribling of Habersham; a son, Alwyn B. Stiles of Athens; three sisters, Mrs. Robert Harper and Mrs. Walter Green Sr., both of Milledgeville, and Mrs. Lillian Saville of Atlanta; a brother, Clifford Stiles of Birmingham, Ala.; 10 grandchildren and a great-grandchild.

In lieu of flowers, the family has asked that contributions be made to the Methodist Children's Home in Decatur.

Bridges Funeral Home is in charge of arrangements.

Memorial Obituary

*Entered Into Eternal Rest
Tuesday, Dec. 11, 1979*

Stiles

Funeral services for Mrs. John C. Stiles were held on Dec. 13 at the Stiles Dimon Chapel of the First United Methodist Church with interment in the Memory Hill Cemetary. Dr. Bevel Jones officiated assisted by the Rev. Wesley Stephens.

Mrs. Stiles died on Dec. 11 at the Athens hospital after a brief illness. She was 88 years old. She was a native of Sheffield, Ala., the daughter of the Rev. Stephen H. and Claudia Yarbrough Dimon. She lived in Athens for the past 40 years. She was a member of the First United Methodist Church and was one of the charter members of the Forum Class.

Mrs. Stiles is survived by one daughter, Mrs. Marion W. Stribling of Habersham, Ga.; one son, Mr. Alwyn B. Stiles of Athens; one sister, Miss Lucile Dimon of Demorest, Ga.; 10 grandchildren, 8 great-grandchildren and three nephews.

Bridges Funeral Home of Athens was in charge of arrangements.

MARION WINTERS STRIBLING
August 03, 1915 – October 11, 2005

Funeral services for Marion Winters Stribling, 90, of Clarkesville, will be held at 11:00 a.m. Thursday, October 13, 2005, at the Clarkesville United Methodist Church with the Rev. Rick Price and Dr. John Bridges officiating. Interment will follow in the Habersham Cemetery.

Mr. Stribling died at his residence on Tuesday, October 11, 2005, following an eight-year battle with multiple myeloma.

Born in Habersham County on August 03, 1915, he was the son of the late Sloan Yowell Stribling, Jr. and Katharine "Kite" Suddath Stribling. He was also preceded in death by a brother, S. Y. Stribling, III, and a sister, Katharine Stribling Bryson.

Mr. Stribling attended grammar school at Habersham Mills School followed by graduation from Demorest High School in 1932. He then attended Clemson University before receiving his draft notice for World War II. He served meritoriously for five years in the U.S. Army in the European Theater of Operations for which he was awarded the Bronze Star, WWII Victory Medal, and European Theater Service Medal. Following his military service, Mr. Stribling began a long and successful career in the textile industry, being appointed Vice-President for Habersham Mills in 1961, and later serving as President from 1965 until his retirement on December 31, 1981. During his textile career, he was President of Georgia Textile Education Foundation, President of American Yarn Spinners Association, and President of Georgia Textile Manufacturers Association.

Mr. Stribling was a long time member of the Clarkesville United Methodist Church where he willingly served in many capacities. His community service included twenty years as Chairman of the Board of Directors of Habersham County Medical Center, a member of the Cornelia Kiwanis Club from which he received the George Hixson Fellow Award in 1998, a 50-year Master Mason and Thirty-Second Degree Shriner, and the Boy Scouts of America Honoree at its American Values Dinner in 2003. He was a member of the Habersham County Historical Society and a past member of the Board of Trustees of Young Harris College.

Survivors include his wife of 58 years, Kathryn Stiles Stribling, of the home and five children and spouses: John and Carol Stribling of Clarkesville, Jack and Brenda Stribling of Roswell, Sloan Stribling of Demorest, Zachary Stribling of Athens, and Mary Stribling of Charlotte, North Carolina. He is also survived by two grandsons and spouse, Jason Stribling of Clarkesville and Jonathan and Jessica Stribling of Demorest, and two granddaughters and spouse, Carrie and Bill Henry of Marietta, and Abbe Stribling of Roswell.

The family will receive friends at the funeral home from 6-9 p.m. on Wednesday. The family is at the residence. Flowers are accepted, or memorials may be made to Clarkesville United Methodist Church; PO Box 365; Clarkesville, GA 30523; or to a charity of one's choice.

McGAHEE-GRIFFIN & STEWART FUNERAL HOME
CORNELIA, GA

IN TRIBUTE

MONDAY, NOVEMBER 23, 2015 · ATHENS BANNER-HERALD

Alwyn Barrington Stiles, Sr.

1918 - 2015

Alwyn Barrington Stiles, Sr. died on November 21, 2015 at the age of 97 in Athens, Ga. He is survived by his sister, Kathryn Stiles Stribling of Athens, five children, nine grandchildren and five great-grandchildren. He was preceded in death in 1982 by his wife of 36 years, Catherine Wingate Stiles.

He was born April 10, 1918 in Acworth, Ga., to the late John Campbell Stiles and the late Mary Haygood Dimon stiles. He moved to Toccoa, Ga., at age 10 and lived with maternal grandparents and aunts until he graduated from Toccoa High School. In 1939, he graduated from the University of Georgia earning a Bachelor's Degree from the School of Forestry. While at UGA he participated in Advanced ROTC and upon graduation fulfilled his active duty commitment as a 2nd Lieutenant, Cavalry.

In February of 1941, he was called to service in the 2nd Armored "Hell on Wheels" Division. His Division fought in North Africa and took part in the invasion of Italy. Three days after D-Day, his unit landed on Juno Beach in Normandy, and later proceeded across France and into Germany. He also participated in the Battle of the Bulge. He was awarded the Bronze Star and other commendations for his service.

After Mr. Stiles' discharge, he returned to Athens to manage the Georgian Hotel. While not completely retiring from the Georgian Hotel, Stiles Apartments and Stiles Properties; he gradually turned daily operations of the business over to his son so he could focus on the activities that he truly enjoyed: University of Georgia Football and spending time in the North Georgia Mountains.

He was a member of the Athens First United Methodist Church, the Gridiron Secret Society and a founding member of the Athens City Club. He spent many years participating and supporting the Boy Scouts of America and in his business career was on the Board of Directors of the Georgia Hotel-Motel Association.

Mr. Stiles is survived by his daughters; Mrs. Alec Poitevint (Doreen) of Bainbridge, Ga., Mrs. Darrel Begnaud (Jane) of Athens, Ga., Mrs. Brian Foster (Lynn) of Savannah, Ga., Mrs. Frank Andrews (Ann) of Clarkesville, Ga., and a son, Alwyn Barrington (Barry) Stiles, Jr. (Karen) of Athens, Ga., six granddaughters, three grandsons, three great-grandsons and 2 great-granddaughters.

Private graveside services are scheduled.

Bridges Funeral Home is in charge of arrangements. www.bridgesfuneral.com.

Please sign the guestbook at onlineathens.com

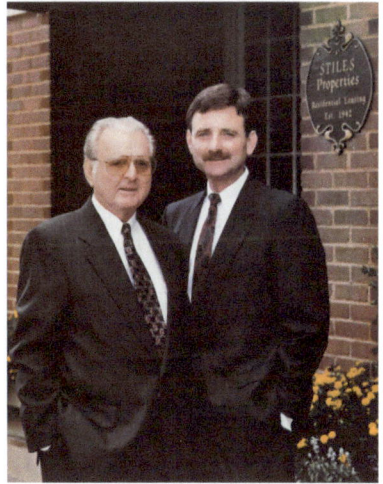

Alwyn Stiles Sr. and son, Alwyn (Barry) Stiles Jr., in front of the Georgian Hotel

Jack and Kathryn at Lake Burton

JACK STILES STRIBLING OBITUARY

Jack Stiles Stribling, 63, of Roswell, GA died February 8, 2014 after a brief battle with cancer.

Formerly of Habersham County, Jack attended North Habersham High School, Young Harris College and served in the United States Navy. He was employed by Rockmart Slate Corporation where he was Vice President of Sales and Chief Operating Officer. Jack was the founding president of the Oakdale-Cumberland Jaycees, served on the Standards Committee of the Atlanta Chapter of the American Red Cross, was an active member of the Polk County Rotary Club serving as Service Project Chairman, and was a two-term Co-President of the nationally recognized Lassiter Band Boosters Association. An avid hunter and fisherman, Jack was devoted to his family and friends and was a champion of his community.

Jack was preceded in death by his father, Marion W. Stribling. He is survived by his wife of 39 years, Brenda Stribling; daughters Carrie Stribling and Abbe Stribling Troyer; granddaughter Annie Henry; his mother Kathryn Stribling; brothers John, Sloan and Zachary Stribling; sister Mary Stribling and nephews Jason and Jonathan Stribling.

A tribute and celebration of his life will be held Saturday, March 8, 2014 at 2:00 p.m. in the Concert Hall on the campus of Lassiter High School in Marietta, GA. In lieu of flowers, the family asks that a donation be made in his name to "Friends of Bulloch, Inc.", P.O. Box 1309, Roswell, GA, or to the Wounded Warrior Project.

SLOAN YOWELL STRIBLING II OBITUARY

Born on Nov. 23, 1951, in Athens, Sloan Stribling was the son of Marion and Kathryn Stribling. He lived his entire life in the Habersham Mills Community. The early portion of his education was in the public schools in Habersham County, and his high school years were spent at The Baylor School in Chattanooga, Tennessee, He attended Piedmont College in Demorest.

Sloan Stribling's 27-year-career with Habersham Mills, culminating in his service as Fiber Department Manager, ended in 1999, when the mill closed, bringing to an end an era of the Stribling family employment in Habersham Mills. From the day the mill opened in 1906, until the day it closed in 1999, there was always at least one member of the Stribling family employed by the mill, and Sloan Stribling was the last family member to carry on that impressive legacy.

Several years as a volunteer firefighter in Habersham County were among his achievements, as well as an enjoyment of the outdoors, especially as an avid hunter and fisherman. He had a special affinity for music and enjoyed singing and playing the guitar. He liked sports, especially football.

He is survived by his mother, Kathryn Stiles Stribling, of Athens; two brothers, John Stribling and wife Carol of Clarkesville, and Zachary Stribling of Athens.

Survivors also include one sister, Mary Stribling of Athens; Left behind also to mourn his passing are his special animal friends, dogs, Punkin, Dixie and Sadie, and cats Tygger and Gizzy.

A Home is built
of peace and love,
And not of wood
or stone,
A place where
understanding lives,
And memories
are sown.

The Stribling Family

SOWING MEMORIES   SINCE 1986

KSS 1986

www.ingramcontent.com/pod-product-compliance
Lightning Source LLC
Chambersburg PA
CBHW040750150426
42813CB00067B/3036/J